D1565792

The Leadership Dilemma in Modern Democracy

NEW HORIZONS IN LEADERSHIP STUDIES

Series Editor: Joanne B. Ciulla
Professor and Coston Family Chair in Leadership and Ethics,
Jepson School of Leadership Studies, University of Richmond, USA
and UNESCO Chair in Leadership Studies,
United Nations International Leadership Academy

This important series is designed to make a significant contribution to the development of leadership studies. This field has expanded dramatically in recent years and the series provides an invaluable forum for the publication of high quality works of scholarship and shows the diversity of leadership issues and practices around the world.

The main emphasis of the series is on the development and application of new and original ideas in leadership studies. It pays particular attention to leadership in business, economics and public policy and incorporates the wide range of disciplines which are now part of the field. Global in its approach, it includes some of the best theoretical and empirical work with contributions to fundamental principles, rigorous evaluations of existing concepts and competing theories, historical surveys and future visions.

Titles in the series include:

Moral Leadership in Action
Building and Sustaining Moral Competence in European Organizations
Edited by Heidi von Weltzien Hoivik

Beyond Rules in Society and Business
Verner C. Petersen

The Moral Capital of Leaders
Why Virtue Matters
Alejo José G. Sison

The Leadership Dilemma in Modern Democracy
Kenneth P. Ruscio

The New Russian Business Leaders
*Manfred F.R. Kets de Vries, Stanislav Shekshnia, Konstantin Korotov
and Elizabeth Florent-Treacy*

Lessons on Leadership by Terror
Finding Shaka Zulu in the Attic
Manfred F.R. Kets de Vries

The Leadership Dilemma in Modern Democracy

Kenneth P. Ruscio

University of Richmond, USA

NEW HORIZONS IN LEADERSHIP STUDIES

Edward Elgar
Cheltenham, UK • Northampton, MA, USA

Published by
Edward Elgar Publishing Limited
The Lypiatts
15 Lansdown Road
Cheltenham
Glos GL50 2JA
UK

Edward Elgar Publishing, Inc.
William Pratt House
9 Dewey Court
Northampton
Massachusetts 01060
USA

Paperback edition 2008

A catalogue record for this book
is available from the British Library

Library of Congress Cataloguing in Publication Data

Ruscio, Kenneth Patrick.
  The leadership dilemma in modern democracy / Kenneth P. Ruscio.
  p. cm. — (New horizons in leadership studies)
  Includes bibliographical references.
  1. Political leadership. 2. Democracy. I. Title. II. Series.

  JC330.3.R87 2004
  303.3'4—dc22

                                                                2004043525

ISBN 978 1 84064 646 7 (cased)
ISBN 978 1 84844 254 2 (paperback)

Printed and bound in Great Britain by MPG Books Ltd, Bodmin, Cornwall

Contents

Acknowledgments

The first glimmers of the idea for this book can be traced to a specific moment. It was a college president's offhand remark. It came at the end of a discussion between just the two of us. I was our college's Dean of Freshmen at the time, and we were meeting as we occasionally did to discuss the latest incident involving one of our socially creative and overly active charges. I forget now whether it was a relatively innocuous violation of policy or a more serious one, but as anyone who has been on college campus for any length of time knows, what freshmen do and what a college wishes they would do often do not coincide. It was my duty to bring their behavior and our aspirations for them into alignment as best I could – to help them, in other words, increase the length of time between impulse and action so that rationality might intrude at least a little into their decision-making. Sometimes, this being one of them, our best efforts were not enough. If a challenge for any leader is to identify where practice falls short of ideals, the Dean of Freshmen's job – not to mention a college president's – is truly a leadership challenge. This was not the first time we had met.

After we solved (in the most generous sense of the word) this particular problem, we moved on to another subject. He had heard that in my other life as a member of our Politics department I had proposed a course on leadership. He was skeptical. You cannot teach leadership, he claimed. It's not a matter of skill or technique. In fact, you can't make any generalization about leadership. He had just come from a meeting of the University's Board of Trustees. 'I was in a room with thirty outstanding leaders,' – he was getting himself worked up now – 'and everyone was different. Old and young. Men and women. Black and white. Tall and short. Extroverted and introverted. Liberal and conservative. Smart and not-so-smart. They had absolutely nothing in common.' He paused for a second. 'Well, yes they did. I suppose if there is one characteristic all good leaders share it is that they are trusted.' He went on to tell a couple of stories from his own college career to reinforce the proposition, but I had taken his point.

As it turned out, I agreed with some of his comments about teaching leadership, but in keeping with the standard rule of thumb among college faculty about deference to a president's wishes, the course went on as planned. But it was this emphasis on trust that had me thinking long after the meeting. Any social scientist or theorist who has studied an issue and become intrigued by it knows how complicated it can be. Otherwise, it wouldn't be of much interest. At the same time, we all need a way to begin organizing our thoughts: a central premise, a simplifying proposition, a starting point, a thesis, or some other kind of entry or gateway into a vast and contested intellectual dialogue. Leadership is about as vast and contested a topic as I had ever encountered. Could trust serve as the focus for an extended inquiry? I was sure that it couldn't be as simple as the president made it out to be, but our conversation took place when polls showing a steep and continuous decline in citizens' trust in government were once again in the headlines. Also, on our own campus, which boasted of a longstanding honor system and a deep historical attachment to two highly regarded public servants, trust was a 'value' or 'tradition' often talked about, which is not to say it was often thought about. The terms were being used very loosely in our parochial community as well as in the nation's political discourse. I decided to look into it more systematically.

What followed was a research agenda that filled my time for a few years, led to a series of articles and essays in academic and opinion journals, and eventually pointed me in the direction of a few other avenues of exploration. One reading led to another. One study seemed to contradict another. New research from psychology, sociology, and even biology was focusing on trust. It was getting complicated, which meant it was getting interesting. This book draws upon many of these themes, although 'upon further reflection' I have revised some of the positions I advanced in those earlier efforts. And the initial focus on trust has given way to a host of related topics. But it was that particular conversation that provided the starting point. Of course, I absolve the president of all responsibility for what he started, though it was in his nature, and perhaps it still is in his blissful retirement, to shoulder whatever blame he could on behalf of others. I do thank him, however.

And there are many, many others to thank. During the course of writing this book, I had the privilege of serving at two institutions of higher education where wise leadership is not merely discussed, studied, debated and taught but constantly on display. At Washington and Lee University, where most of this was written: Larry Peppers and Larry Boetsch, Robert Strong and the members of the Politics Department, as well as my good interdisciplinary friends Harlan Beckley and Lad Sessions. At the Jepson School of Leadership Studies at the University of Richmond: all my new colleagues, faculty and staff, and especially Joanne Ciulla for her patience, encouragement, and editorial assistance along the way.

And, of course, my family: my father and late mother who were more confident than I that this book would eventually arrive; Matthew, my son, whose eyes now roll reflexively at the mere mention of Thomas Jefferson and leadership; and most of all, Kim, my wife, whose extraordinary self-discipline has enabled her to control the eye-rolling reflex, at least most of the time.

Introduction: The Dilemma of Leadership and Democracy

The theory of democracy does not treat leaders kindly. Suspicion of rulers, concern over their propensity to abuse power in their own self-interest, the need to hold them accountable, and the belief that legitimate power is lodged originally in the people and granted to leaders only with severe contingencies, all are fixed stars in the democratic galaxy. In many respects, democracy came about as the remedy to the problem of leadership, at least as defined by a long list of political philosophers. Fear of leadership is a basic justification for democratic forms of government.

Yet it is impossible to imagine a strong, healthy democracy without leaders. A central objective of this study is to recover those elements of democratic thought that acknowledge the indispensable, fundamental, and positive contributions of leaders. If we want vibrant, dynamic and progressive democracies, we need to be very clear about how we expect leaders to perform, the demands we can appropriately place on them, and their responsibilities to the polity and the citizens.

Making the case for a particular kind of leadership requires first making the case for a particular kind of democracy. Leadership theory in the context of democratic politics is a subset of democratic theory. Chapter 1 explains why claims about the obligations of leaders in a democracy are also unavoidably normative arguments about democracy as well. Chapters 2 and 3 go on to examine a couple of the specific responsibilities of democratic leaders. They should foster and ensure reasoned public debate. And they must establish the kind of relationship with citizens that ensure trust. 'Public reason' and 'trust' are actually not necessary for *any* form of democratic leadership, but they are necessary for the version presented in these pages. Chapters 4 through 7 build a sustained argument for one more basic leadership responsibility that is at the core of the kind of democracy I defend: the promotion of the public interest over private interest. That also is a contested claim, one based on an assumption that there is a common good that is something more than the mere accumulation of all the private interests in society. A theory of democracy based on such an assumption will have different things to say about leadership than one based on the assumption that the common good is an elusive, artificial, and unrealistic goal.

The intersection of leadership theory and democratic theory is at the heart of this study. And while it may seem at first self-evident that a normative theory of leadership requires critical engagement with democratic thought, the literature on political leadership in democracies rarely draws from political philosophy in any systematic or explicit manner.

That could very well be because democratic theorists only occasionally focus directly on leaders, per se, although much of what they say has enormous implications for how we enable officials to lead while constraining their discretion and scope of authority. Whatever the explanation, students of leadership typically overlook political philosophy, the historical development of democratic thought, the analytical constructs it provides, and the competing perspectives it brings to ongoing debates about the legitimacy of political power.

There are two boundaries to the project. The first should already be obvious, but given the current state of the literature it bears emphasis. I am addressing political leadership. There are undoubtedly similarities among leaders in different sectors of society – in business, science, religion, and education. But the broad-brush approach – the 'seven habits of highly effective leaders' model – obscures the unique demands placed on public officials. In the political sphere particular rather than general obligations apply, especially in democracies governed by a constitution, which accords a certain status to the individual and makes collective action problematic. That is why democratic theory, which presents justifications and principles underlying normative beliefs, becomes so essential. What may not yet be obvious, but I hope will soon become so, is that carving out a political realm distinct from other realms has significant implications for the model of leadership I endorse.

And that leads to the second boundary. To underscore my claim that assertions about political leadership cannot be made apart from claims for a preferred form of democracy, I will draw from liberal theory – liberal in the broad, historical sense of individualism, freedom, equality and tolerance and limited governmental power; liberal in the sense of allowing individuals to seek their own version of the good life bound by the constraints of justice. The dilemma of leadership in a democracy, to put a finer point on it, is the process of constraining rulers because we fear them, even as we empower them to lead society in its collective pursuit of its noblest and most ambitious aspirations.

The study might therefore be read on two levels. One is to ask what contemporary liberal democratic theory tells us about leadership. In a polity animated by liberal precepts, what are the duties and obligations of leaders? Liberal theorists may evaluate this project by whether it accurately presents a view of leadership in accord with well-established liberal tenets. Those critical of liberal theory may approach it differently – that is, to see this project as simply an example of how one strand of political thought might be mined for insights into leadership. If communitarians responded with their own version, or if postmoderns or other critics of liberalism retaliated by showing how their versions of leadership would look very different, or if devotees of the ancients reminded us of the early writings on statesmanship and rulership, this project will have achieved one of its main goals.

These boundaries circumscribe the project but not nearly enough. Far too much territory remains under the heading of liberal political leadership. There are many versions of liberalism, and the realm of the political has itself been the scene of many recent boundary disputes. To bring focus and order to the discussion, I have focused on three central themes. Certainly there might be others. Certainly they might be cut differently. But any excursion into liberal thought with the intent of identifying premises for leadership would inevitably encounter at least these concepts in one form or another. Moreover, as I hope to show, they have relevance for present-day debates over the state of politics in society. The following sections briefly state these concepts:

Public Reason

In a polity derived from the just powers of the governed, where the governed differ in their values and beliefs, there will inevitably be conflict. The management of conflict to arrive at collective action is a fundamental task of leaders. But the way in which conflict is managed is at least one distinguishing feature of liberal polities. We must be willing to live with others who differ from us; the end of politics is not the imposition of the good life for all but the creation of conditions that allow each to achieve his version of the good life without being unjust to others. Action to solve common problems stops well short of the imposition of a single version of the received wisdom. Conflict is permanent, and therefore so is politics.

Even so, we must cooperate and coexist with others who differ from us in substantial ways. Rawls puts the problem squarely: 'How is it possible for there to exist over time a just and stable society of free and equal citizens, who remain profoundly divided by reasonable religious, philosophical and moral doctrines?'[1] One answer is that they must justify their reasons for a particular course of action, if that action calls upon the coercive power of the state, in terms that are understandable to others. They must reason publicly. They must understand if not always endorse the positions of those they live with. Leaders must not only do the same (indeed, their obligation is greater) but they must also create the conditions that allow for public deliberation.

Trust as a Political Virtue

A central issue for the contemporary, liberal, administrative state is balancing two imperatives. The *political* imperative requires public officials to be accountable. Perhaps the primary method of ensuring accountability is to limit authority. Those who govern cannot simply declare a course of action. They are checked and balanced; their powers are often divided. Richard Neustadt reports on a now-famous observation from Harry Truman, who looked on bemused as the office of the presidency was passed on to Eisenhower the former general. 'Poor Ike. He'll sit here and he'll say, "Do this! Do that!" and nothing will happen. It won't be a bit like the Army. He'll find it very frustrating.'[2] Constitutional government has higher priorities than efficiency, and one of the primary reasons is an inherent suspicion or even mistrust of those who find themselves in positions of power.

But as the scope of government expanded, so did the administrative tasks that require discretion and flexibility, thus creating a *managerial* imperative very different from the political one. The key to resolving the tension between these two imperatives is trust.[3] To declare that mistrust is a central premise of liberal polities is not to declare that trust has no place. One of the purposes of this study is to recover the significance of trust in leaders as an element of liberal theory. To do so, however, requires a distinction between the kind of trust we develop in our personal lives among friends and families and the trust we have in our public lives as citizens. Political trust, I will argue, is not the same as personal trust. A political virtue is in some important respects different from personal virtue.[4] To develop a theory of liberal political leadership, we need to clarify why trust is important, what form it takes, and how it is nurtured within an institutional structure based on an assumption that power can be misused.

The Possibility of a Common Good

Often in political theory, very basic assumptions carry enormous implications for how we envision government. Consider the simple question whether individuals act in their self-interest. Of course they do some of the time or maybe even most of the time. But do they always? Are they ever able to sacrifice self-interest in the name of some greater duty or obligation? Is there something in principle called the public interest? Does it consist merely of the arithmetic summation of all individual interests or is the whole greater than the sum of its parts?

There is indeed a common good that transcends individual interests – and a model of leadership based on that assumption differs markedly from one constrained by a rigid assumption of self-interested behavior. A search for a common good obligates leaders to act differently than they would if their main obligation were only to respond to and balance separate and competing interests. That argument requires some adventurous forays into discussions of human nature, a topic that has engendered some of the most contested claims in political theory. This inquiry surely won't settle the matter, but it will demonstrate the importance of revealing the assumptions we use to construct our preferred models of leadership. Many arguments about the responsibilities of public officials can be traced back to disagreements on some of these basic assumptions.

Readers familiar with contemporary debates among democratic theorists will recognize a number of highly charged assertions in the preceding paragraphs. It will be clear to them already that I am presenting *a* version of liberal political leadership, not *the* version. I will locate my claims in the writings of readily recognized theorists – Machiavelli, Locke, and Montesquieu from earlier days; Hamilton, Madison, Jay, and Jefferson closer to our day; and from our day Rawls especially. Of course, those theorists and others mentioned throughout these pages do not form a coherent package. They differ sharply on key points and the emphasis they place on the precepts they do hold in common. But they do share a strong intellectual tradition in political thought – a belief in the efficacy of government, as well as a fear that it can constrain individual autonomy. In contemporary times, the challenge to liberal thought comes from a variety of sources, particularly those such as communitarians, feminists and postmodernists who believe that liberalism, with its emphasis on individualism, rights, and procedural justice, negates the conditions which are required for it to flourish.[5] In liberal regimes, the argument goes, individual choice is glorified to the detriment of the formation of community; procedures are given a higher priority than any substantive good; and the reluctance to assert any firm values results in weakening of the civil virtues necessary for a healthy vibrant society.

This inquiry defends the liberal tradition but admittedly falls into the camp of what might be called 'chastened liberalism.' Peter Berkowitz is one of its current champions and his work is characterized by the concession that the critics have hit their mark and raised difficult issues, even though he believes that in the end they have failed to penetrate the core beliefs of liberal thought. The appropriate strategy for liberals is to recognize that indeed liberalism embodies inherent tensions and to rework their analysis to take into account the sociological conditions of contemporary society. To take an example particularly relevant to this discussion of leadership, liberals are (almost instinctively) reluctant to speak of virtues for fear that the perceived need to cultivate democratic virtues implicates the power of government to do so. At the same time, however, as Berkowitz convincingly shows, liberal societies depend on the existence of several critical virtues, such as civility, toleration, and respect for difference. Liberal theorists traditionally resolved the dilemma by placing faith in the ability of extra-governmental institutions – church, family, associations, and in some cases the market – to cultivate those virtues. But as Berkowitz points out, times change. 'Liberalism today no longer has easy access to the beliefs, practices, and institutions from which the makers of modern liberalism could once confidently draw to sustain virtue.'[6] In light of the current erosion of what might be called civil society, perhaps liberals need to be more assertive in their discussion of matters such as virtue, community, and the beneficial involvement of government.

> The practical and pressing challenge faced by liberal democracies today is to discover not how to become a different or better kind of regime, but how to make themselves better at defending liberal principles and achieving purposes for which liberal states are formed. This cause can be advanced by liberals who learn to take more responsibility for cultivating the qualities of mind and character whose necessity for the preservation of liberal states can be shown by theory, but whose existence, theory also suggests, cannot be presupposed by practice.[7]

Virtue of a particular kind is necessary for leadership in liberal democracies.

To introduce the term 'virtue' into a discussion of political leadership, especially one that draws from liberal political philosophy, runs the risk of misinterpretation. In the popular press and a climate of the political scandal of the day, lack of virtue becomes a too convenient weapon against public officials whose policies raise objections. Bad moral character is a vicious accusation. When used as a proxy for a disagreement with someone's policies, it raises the stakes of political debate in a manner that does little to improve it. A bad person without virtue is worse than a bad policymaker or an incompetent leader.

Ironically, in public discourse these days the charge of bad conduct, while raising the stakes, is often a less demanding argument to make than addressing the typically complicated details of public policy. Public deliberation suffers when virtue is the first and only measure of a public official's capacity for office. Rather than elevating public debate, it cheapens and corrupts it, makes it more salacious, and reduces it to facile and righteous personal condemnation of individuals.

That is not to say that virtue in political leaders is inconsequential or that ethical vigilance of leaders is wasted effort. Quite the contrary. It is fundamental to the theory of political leadership I propose. But in liberal political philosophy, which grants individuals significant autonomy to make their own choices about the good life, thereby reserving for them a realm of the private off-limits under most circumstances to public intrusion, virtue must be discussed in fairly precise and significantly complex ways. Because liberalism distinguishes between public and private life – because, that is, the state can intrude upon private decisions only when demanding criteria are met – a distinction between public and private virtue is worth some attention. When we speak of virtuous conduct of individuals in their public capacities – citizens as citizens and leaders as leaders – what specific virtues do we have in mind? As citizens and leaders, as opposed to parents, church members, executives, professionals, workers, or whatever, what good behaviors should they display, and what are the virtues – those innate feelings, capacities, and habits – that ensure desirable behavior?

To anticipate some of the arguments to come, but without delving into the details, the central virtues of sympathy, impartiality, and tolerance are among those that come together to fashion a kind of disposition toward service to others. Sympathy, because it enables an individual to understand the needs of others and, to some degree, enables leaders to place themselves in the positions of others. Impartiality, because the ability to separate an individual's claim from the person making the claim is of vital importance in democracies that place a priority on fairness and equality before the law. Tolerance, because leaders must respect views different from theirs even when they do not agree with or endorse the views. Stephen Macedo's litany is helpful: 'broad sympathies, self-critical reflectiveness, a willingness to experiment, to try and accept new things, self-control and active, autonomous self-development, an appreciation of inherited social ideals, an attachment and even an altruistic regard for one's fellow liberal citizens.'[8] Political leadership, particularly leadership in a liberal democracy, is not the pursuit of self-interest through a different and strategically advantageous position of power. Even more so than in other constructions of the good state, it is a duty and responsibility to serve others through the pursuit of the public interest.

As Macedo and others have persuasively argued, the core tenets of liberal political theory are not neutral with respect to virtue. Nor can liberals safely claim that personal virtue has nothing to do with public or civic virtue. But by carefully delineating the roles and responsibilities of political leaders and by carefully delineating the range of activities that fall into the realm of the public, liberals have unavoidably also carved out a range of virtues appropriate for those circumscribed arenas. Can a theory of liberal political leadership make room for a discussion of virtue? Unquestionably. Indeed, it is central to this book. But it must employ careful distinctions and proceed with modest constraint.

Notes

1. John Rawls, *Political Liberalism* (New York: Columbia University Press, 1996), 4.
2. Richard E. Neustadt, *Presidential Power and the Modern Presidents: The Politics of Leadership from Roosevelt to Reagan* (New York: Free Press, 1991), 10.
3. Kenneth P. Ruscio, 'Trust in the Administrative State,' *Public Administration Review* 57, 5 (September/October, 1997), 454–458.
4. Kenneth P. Ruscio, 'Jay's Pirouette, or Why Political Trust Is Not the Same as Personal Trust,' *Administration & Society* 31, 5 (November 1999), 639–657.
5. There is a large literature. For a classic statement most often interpreted as a communitarian analysis, see Michael Sandel, *Liberalism and the Limits of Justice*, second edition (New York: Cambridge University Press, 1998). A liberal response directly to the critics is Stephen Holmes, *The Anatomy of Antiliberalism* (Cambridge, MA: Harvard University Press, 1996).
6. Peter Berkowitz, *Virtue and the Making of Modern Liberalism* (Princeton, NJ: Princeton University Press, 1999), 173.
7. Ibid., 184.
8. Stephen Macedo, *Liberal Virtues: Citizenship, Virtue, and Community in Liberal Constitutionalism* (Oxford: Clarendon Press, 1990), 272.

1. Why Democratic Theory Is Essential for Leadership Theory

In the current political climate, a study of leadership and democracy would seem to have an abundance of problems to solve and examples to discuss. It is tempting to explore how the 'politics of personal destruction' limits the ability of democracies to attract the most talented leaders, or the ways in which wealth determines the outcomes of political campaigns, or the apparent inability of rival parties to raise the level of public debate. Something, it seems, is not quite right with the condition of democracy, as some very provocative and insightful commentaries have explained. Consider, for example, Alan Wolfe's 1989 book, *Whose Keeper? Social Science and Moral Obligation*, one of the first to refocus attention on the decline in civil society and its importance in moderating the acquisitiveness fostered by economic markets and the coercive tendencies inherent in governmental actions.[1] Or Jean Bethke Elshtain's *Democracy on Trial*, a veritable call to arms, reminding us that individualism and rights without obligation and a sense of mutual interdependence eventually lead to an impoverished polity.[2] Or the now well-known work of Robert Putnam who warned that democracy suffers when social capital declines – when we 'bowl alone' instead of in leagues; when we neglect our Rotary clubs, chambers of commerce, PTAs, Little Leagues, soccer clubs, and other civic organizations; when we form our opinions while passively watching television instead of engaging our fellow citizens in debate and being challenged by them; when, in general, we lose sight of our obligations as citizens to join with others in common cause.[3]

Consider, also, the extensive data we now have on the decline in political participation, such as voting, working for a candidate, or simply being aware of issues and what candidates stand for.[4] Or the annual surveys of college freshmen which each year portray students as more and more cynical about politics, unconcerned or ignorant about the effect it has on their lives, and highly skeptical about their ability to change society for the better through political engagement.[5] Only one-third of those between 18 and 29 vote in presidential elections and less than one-fifth vote in congressional elections. More than one-half does not believe that it matters who is president, and less than seven percent have directly participated in a political campaign. Historically, youth have been less involved than their elders in civic and political life, but youth today are far less involved than their parents and grandparents were when they were young. It is a pattern that does not bode well for the future.[6]

E.J. Dionne's bluntly titled but astutely argued *Why Americans Hate Politics* made a provocative claim.

> Over the last three decades, the faith of the American people in their democratic institutions has declined, and Americans have begun to doubt their ability to improve the world through politics…Americans view politics with boredom and detachment. For most of us, politics is increasingly abstract, a spectator sport barely worth watching. Election campaigns generate less excitement than ever and are dominated by television commercials, direct mail, polling, and other approaches that treat individual voters not as citizens deciding their nation's fate, but as mere collections of impulses to be stroked and soothed…Americans hate politics as it now practiced because we have lost all sense of the public good … A nation that hates politics will not long survive as a democracy.[7]

The analyses of Wolfe, Elshtain, Putnam, and Dionne form the backdrop for this study. There is cause for concern, despite the apparent resurgence in national purpose and the rising trust in government occasioned by the responsiveness of public officials to the terrorist attacks of September 11, 2001. But contemporary critiques of democracy, no matter how insightful, pay almost no attention to the political philosophical foundations of leadership. This work is an attempt to fill that void, but it does so by adopting the very different strategy of stepping back from today's events, not by immersing ourselves into them. If it sheds light on the current state of democracy, it will be because it has removed itself from the present to examine the complex and confusing legacy handed down to us from a number of influential, insightful, and imaginative thinkers. Ideas do matter. The language that we use to express our beliefs, principles, and opinions has a history. But the intricacies of the arguments of our intellectual forbears have been lost along the way, so that modern writers appropriate their statements selectively to support their own polemics.

To be more accurate, we should say that the legacy is really a set of legacies. The writers and thinkers of earlier times emphasized different aspects of democracy – sometimes glorifying the generosity and wisdom of the common man, other times bemoaning his selfishness and ignorance; sometimes placing faith in the virtue of leaders, other times issuing dire warnings about their vices and ambition for power; sometimes optimistic that we can achieve a common good, other times resigned to an endless divisiveness and factionalism.

As a result, we are not always consistent in diagnosing our present situation or proposing remedies for the condition of modern politics. It is especially problematic when the prescription for what ails democracy is blithely presented as 'better leadership.' If we think leadership can solve our problems, or if we want better leaders, we need first to understand the particular forms of democracy we endorse. Different principles of democracy – different aspirations – impose distinctly different kinds of obligations and responsibilities on leaders. Calls for better leadership in their generality often mask conflicting preferences for particular forms of politics. We cannot prescribe 'better' leadership until we clearly specify what kind of democracy we aspire to having. Developing a normative theory of democratic leadership requires tapping into some of the most basic disputes about the forms and principles of democracy.

That is not an easy task. The concept of leadership has a hard time fitting into political theories of liberal democracy. The mere mention of it worries defenders of individual liberty, since it implies the use of power to achieve collective ends, and that implies coercion. Leadership often means persuading people to do something they originally may not have wanted to do or perhaps even fashioning policies that may require them to do something they will never want to do, so it is seen as a threat rather than a friend to liberty, part of the process of contracting the scope of permissible behavior rather than expanding it. That is one reason why virtually all modern democratic theorists have to address the problem of how public officials can lead society to collective ends without intruding upon individual autonomy. They draw a distinction between power and authority, for example, or devote a lot of attention to methods of accountability that will protect citizens when officials exercise their discretion a little too energetically. But the point is that leadership and liberty have to be reconciled. They do not naturally fall in line side by side.

Leadership also worries defenders of equality. It implies the selection of individuals with characteristics – skills, talents, or virtues – that set them apart from others. Leaders are not, by definition, everyone. On the basis of some set of criteria they must be distinguished from those unwilling or unable to be leaders – leaving aside for the moment the challenging issue of who actually does the distinguishing. Leadership may be inevitable when people gather to solve their collective problems, but in a democracy that is not the same as saying it is desirable. When democratic theorists are not focusing on the problem of liberty, they therefore must turn their attention to reconciling love of equality with the need for leadership. The 'rule of law' is one method of recourse. In the eyes of the law everyone is equal. No person, no matter the formal position or title, is exempt from it. But as is the case with liberty, the theory must do some work. Equality and leadership won't fall together if left to their own devices.

And so democratic theorists have wrestled with a seemingly intractable problem – the inescapable need for leadership of some sort, if only for the pragmatic reason of organizing a collective effort, and the unavoidable way in which leadership threatens the highest values of basic democracy. For some political philosophers, the effort is simply too daunting. Benjamin Barber is one whose 'passion for democracy' (the title of one of his books) makes him uncomfortable with enthusiastic endorsements of bold and visionary leadership. Strong leadership, in his view, weakens democracy. 'It is that the very virtues that make for leadership have attenuated the skills and capacities that constitute citizenship. A too responsible leadership can make for an irresponsible citizenry; an overly vigorous executive can reduce citizens to passive observers whose main activity is applause,' he writes. 'A leader strong enough to do everything we would like done for us is strong enough to deprive us of the capacity to do anything at all for ourselves.'[8] There are only two options: more leadership or more democracy. For Barber the choice is clear. Active and engaged citizens rather than forceful and energetic leaders make for the better polity.

But the story gets complicated. Even as democrats have looked warily upon leadership in theory, they have accepted it in practice. Like Irving Babbitt, William Bryce and other on-the-scene observers of democracy, they must come to terms with the realization that 'democracy will stand or fall on the quality of its leadership.'[9] As Arthur Schlesinger explains so well:

> An adequate democratic theory must recognize that democracy is not self-executing; that leadership is not the enemy of self-government but the means of making it work; that followers have their own stern obligation, which is to keep leaders within rigorous constitutional bounds; and that Caesarism is more often produced by the failure of feeble governments than by the success of energetic ones.[10]

History has provided us with examples of disastrous democratic leadership, to be sure, but also with enough examples of democracies that have emerged stronger as a result of leadership not so obviously at odds with the principles of freedom and equality.

The standard way of reconciling this tension in democratic theory – of maximizing the possibility of successful leadership while minimizing the threats to democracy – is to fashion intricate institutional designs, features of which have become so familiar to us in modern times that we have forgotten the basic reasons why they developed in the first place. For example, we divide the tasks of governing into separate institutions in such a way that even if one flawed person were to succumb to the temptations of power the overall damage to liberty and equality would be well contained. Or we distinguish between the individual who holds an office at any given moment from the powers and responsibilities assigned to the office. The authority goes with the formally defined position, and remains there when the incumbent moves on.

This general strategy of institutional design has a vital place in democratic theory. But in its basic form standing alone as the only answer to the tension, it is a form of surrender to the less appealing characteristics of the human psyche. It essentially downgrades leadership, reducing it to nothing more than the fulfillment of a certain institutional role and the expression of the interests assigned to that position. Democratic leadership requires something more, especially if – as I will argue in this study – public reason and careful deliberation, political trust, and the possibility of a common good are central features of a vigorous, healthy, and vibrant democracy. Enlightened statesmen will not always be at the helm, but that does not mean we should be indifferent to the choice between enlightened or unenlightened ones, backing ourselves into the position that we can do just as well with the bunglers and the corrupt as we can with the wise and judicious because of our ingenious institutional safeguards. Can a democracy make room for an energetic, legitimate, and just leadership compatible with the principles of equality and liberty? Or are democracy and leadership simply irreconcilable?

The practice of leadership will always be in tension with the theory of democracy. A fascination with leaders does indeed divert one's eyes from the true source of legitimacy and authority in a democracy, an active and engaged citizenry. On the other hand, a rejection of leadership is implicitly a rejection of democracy. How else can democracy be justified except in terms of people taking control of their collective destiny? And how else can leadership be justified except in terms of helping society in that endeavor – of following the legacies of Machiavelli (at least his more benign observations), Montesquieu, Madison, and others that the choices we make, not fate and fortune, shape our future? A normative theory of democratic leadership must perch itself on the fine line between embracing the good that virtuous leaders can provide and fearing the damage the less virtuous have the potential to inflict.

The course of modern democratic thought is really one of balancing the image of the leader as positive change-agent who elevates other individuals to higher moral planes of collective goodness against the image of leaders as congenitally manipulative power-seekers, who by their very willingness to assume positions of leadership betray an ambition that renders them even more prone to deviousness than the people they lead. As Algernon Sydney warned,

> Men are so subject to vices, and passions, that they stand in need of some restraints in every condition; but especially when they are in power. The rage of a private man may be pernicious to one or few of his neighbors; but the fury of an unlimited prince would rive whole nations into ruin. And those very men, who lived modestly when they had little power, have often proved the most savage of monsters when they thought nothing able to resist their rage.[11]

On the other hand, 'the aim of every political constitution is,' James Madison wrote, 'or ought to be, first to obtain for rulers men who possess most wisdom to discern, and most virtue to pursue, the common good of the society.'[12] A

flaw in the human condition makes one type of leadership regrettably necessary. A yearning for something better makes the other version desirable. The
ebb of one version and the flow of the other is the dilemma of leadership in
modern democracy.

It is also the theme of this book. Although a healthy skepticism of leadership can never be far from the thoughts of democratic theorists, a pathological
obsession with it results in a democracy too cramped and unimaginative. It
can lead to precisely the opposite of that which Barber and other ardent democrats wish to avoid: a democracy of solitary and atomistic individuals striving
for nothing more than to be left alone, unwilling to commit to any cause beyond themselves. That is not democracy at its best. We need to identify and
elaborate upon the crucial elements of a normative theory of leadership that
supports a democracy of greater aspirations.

Debates about the current condition of democracy skim past the question
of leadership. We hear a great deal about the lack of civility in public discourse, the decline of trust in institutions and public officials, the pursuit of
self-interest by citizens and their representatives, the apparent incapacity of
the political system to address long-range problems, and the futility of any
form of political engagement. Civil society appears to be anything but civil,
and public deliberation as a means of resolving differences seems a hopeless
ideal, nice in theory but wholly unachievable in practice. Democracy, as
Elshtain warns, is on trial, challenged by 'deepening cynicism; the growth of
corrosive forms of isolation, boredom, and despair; the weakening, in other
words, of the world known as democratic civil society, a world of groups and
associations and ties that bind.'[13]

The matter of leadership is implicit in these discussions, or when it is made
explicit it comes in one of two forms: either platitudinous observations about
the need for integrity, boldness and vision; or crass, simplistic misappropria-
tions of complex and sophisticated political theories. When Jonathan Rauch's
otherwise shrewd critique of politics as systematically driven by organized
groups ends with a plea for 'that most personal and fickle of counterforces:
political leadership,' we sense that his analytical powers and narrative skills
have exhausted themselves.[14] The very premise of his argument was that everyone, citizens and leaders alike, is inescapably complicit in the problem he
calls 'demosclerosis.' When Dick Morris, President Clinton's erstwhile advi-
sor, tries to justify his view of politics as merely a modern version of
Machiavelli's *The Prince*, he reveals not only his perverse notion of ethics but
also his tendency to mangle political philosophy in service of his cause.[15]
When democracy is in trouble or suffering from one malady or another, leadership often receives the blame. Yet it soon becomes the solution as well,
revealing our limited understanding of the connections between leadership
and democracy.

Although it may seem self-evident that theories of leadership are embedded within theories of democracy, modern discussions of leadership proceed otherwise, as if untethered to political philosophy. One consequence is that while we aggressively debate timeless questions of democratic theory, such as the terms of engagement in the public sphere and the condition of civil society, we root around aimlessly when discussing leadership, unaware that disputes in democratic theory inevitably lead to disputes about the nature of leadership. The effect is not unlike one of the characters described in a Richard Russo novel as 'not profoundly stupid' but missing 'his fair share of nuances.'[16] That fits the state of our theories on political leadership – not completely off the mark but lacking appreciation for subtlety and complexity.

For example, when someone claims that democracy requires civility, what additional claims about democratic leadership are also being made? Stephen Carter's provocative book provides some clues. We must first accept that there will be continuous disagreement in a democracy, constant dialogue instead of final consensus, a form of politics marked by commitment to principles, to be sure, but also a willingness to learn from others. 'Civil listening' is one of Carter's ideals. 'The function of debate in a truly civil society is not only to prevail; the function is to allow the best idea to win out. Therefore,' he concludes, 'no matter how certain I may be that I am right, unless I give you a genuine and open opportunity to persuade me of my errors, I cannot seriously expect you to give me a genuine and open opportunity to persuade you of yours.'[17] Leaders presumably should model this public etiquette while creating conditions that enable and encourage citizens to act in the same manner.

Perhaps – but to Alan Wolfe, one of Carter's critics, the answer is not so clear. Civility is only one of many virtues and when virtues come into conflict we have to assign priority to one over another. In the private realm of family and friends, civility may frequently if not always take precedence. In the public world of argument and debate, however, fighting injustice and standing for principle may at times trump civility. Sometimes we show respect for others by attacking the insufficiency of their ideas.[18] While Wolfe would not dismiss the benefit of civility, he does help us understand that our vision of democratic politics – what we imagine its purposes to be – inevitably leads to discussion of how we wish leaders to behave. The leadership behavior we endorse depends, that is, on the kind of democracy we want.

Another example raises a related but somewhat different question. In the late 1980s, when the budget deficit framed virtually all political debate and elected officials seemed incapable of making hard choices, a soon-to-be-retired senator rose to address his colleagues. John Danforth, a Republican from Missouri, was dismayed over his colleagues' refusal to rein in entitlement spending. Fearing the fiscal burden that would eventually be placed on future generations and judging that to be a classic case of injustice, the senator blamed the inaction on the electoral imperative – the overriding impulse to placate short-term demands from constituents at the cost of long-term benefits. Speaking extemporaneously and indignantly with a passion that revealed his frustration, he continued:

> Deep down in our hearts we know that we have bankrupted America and that we have given our children a legacy of bankruptcy. We have been so intent on getting ourselves elected that year after year we have told the people that they get their choice between more benefits and lower taxes .... The problem is that we have hurt America – quite intentionally we have hurt America, for the purposes of getting ourselves elected. We have told Americans that they should feel sorry for themselves. We have told them we can give them something for nothing. We have told them we can reduce taxes and we can increase benefits, and the numbers do not add up, and people want to believe that this is not a problem.[19]

Danforth's particular plaint about the budget is beside the point. What does matter is his accusation that public officials fail to sacrifice their own interest (in this case electoral success) in the name of what they determine to be in public interest. In addition, he suggests that officials have a responsibility to educate the public about their choices – to lead rather than mislead.

His sentiments have an undeniable appeal, and I shall take them up later. Still, direct responsiveness to constituents should not be too quickly dismissed. After all, the justification for elections as a means of accountability is that officials will and should be influenced by the incentive to please those they represent. Even more to the point, can we realistically expect representatives to ignore their own basic self-interest in the name of some amorphously defined public good any more than we can expect citizens to override theirs? In the view of many democratic theorists, interests rather than ideas or principles drive politics.[20] Some go even further. Interests actually check the unbridled and impulsive passions. They should be not only tolerated but embraced. Constructing theories of leadership without a realistic appraisal of human nature, some would surely argue, is to create an untenable portrayal of the responsibilities of leaders. Of course, the features of human nature, let alone their implications for politics, are very much open to debate, but that is precisely the point. Implicit in Danforth's version of leadership is one view, a view with appeal but a contested one that must be defended.

A final example. In what is surely one of the most revealing portraits of modern-day, street-level, genuine retail politics, Buzz Bissinger writes of the tenure of Ed Rendell, mayor of Philadelphia in the mid-1990s. Rendell faced enormous constraints, including a rapidly deteriorating fiscal climate, exacerbated by self-reinforcing trends. The more people left the city because of crime, loss of jobs, and inferior education, the smaller the tax base, and the greater the inability to rectify the very problems that caused people to leave, thereby touching off still more departures. As industries historically important to the city's economy closed or moved, Rendell tried to fill the void by attracting shoppers and tourists, only to be charged with ignoring the city's traditional neighborhoods. The job became all-consuming. His daily schedule was a series of events ranging from phone calls and meetings with the President and Cabinet Secretaries to appearances at funerals for slain policemen to dancing with mascots for companies who donated small change to minor civic events. His office became the repository for demands completely irreconcilable. Bissinger's portrait is unabashedly sympathetic. Rendell 'knew better than anyone else how politics worked, the persona and the aura of the job subsuming everything else. People saw him as the mayor, always the mayor, never as a man who might have brushes with insecurity and sadness and even frailty .... [H]e wondered whether the standards for politicians were just impossible to ever fully meet.'[21] Bissinger continues:

> He was the embodiment of a public man, utterly defined by his place in the public eye and the way in which the public reacted to him, and the private acts which define a life – family, friendships, religious faith – seemed of little sustaining moment to him. Whatever it was, wherever it was, he hated being outside the circle. But in the elusive definition of what it means to be a public servant, no one else came closer to the ideals that the concept represents. He gave of himself tirelessly, and his motive wasn't pure self-aggrandizement or strokes of the ego, nor was it mere obligation. He was hardly a student of urban history and urban planning. He had no grand theory that could be explained on paper. But he understood exactly what a city was about – sounds and sights and smells, all the different sense, held together by the spontaneity of choreography, each day, each hour, each minute different from the previous one.[22]

In the canonical literature on leadership, there is a distinction drawn between transactional and transformational leadership. The former refers to leadership based on transactions between leaders and followers, agreements or bargains that promise mutually beneficial results. 'If you vote for me and provide me with a position,' a politician will say, 'I promise to fulfill your interests.' By contrast, transformational leadership offers a new way of looking at the world. Leaders provide not bargains but ideas, hopes, and aspirations.[23] The distinction (which I have unfairly simplified) is a useful one. It has contributed to our understanding. Yet one wonders whether it applies in any way to Rendell's case. As he came to embody the city, to the point of losing any sense of a private life outside of his official role, as he worked tirelessly to overcome the constraints and usher in a new vision for the city, was he transformational? Or was his leadership better understood as an endless attempt to balance demands of a heterogeneous group of constituents? Rendell was both transactional and transformational and therefore was neither. The demands of leadership in a democracy call for bargains and transactions – hard, cold tit-for-tat tradeoffs – but within a context of goals, purposes and objectives. Certainly the most influential leadership theorists, such as James MacGregor Burns, acknowledge that successful leaders must be both. But the complex view often gives way to the simplistic: that leaders tend to be one or the other.

And so our understanding of leadership is confused – one of the most observed phenomena, as Burns has noted, but one of the least understood. One strategy for reducing the confusion is to examine specific parts or components of leadership – in this case, public reason, trust, and the common good.

Notes

1. Alan Wolfe, *Whose Keeper? Social Science and Moral Obligation* (Berkeley: University of California Press, 1989).
2. Jean Bethke Elshtain, *Democracy on Trial* (New York: Basic Books, 1995).
3. Robert D. Putnam, *Bowling Alone: The Collapse and Revival of American Community* (New York: Simon & Schuster, 2000). Putnam's work has been at the center of the discussion in recent years on social capital. See also his 'The Prosperous Community' Social Capital and Public Life, *American Prospect*, 13 (Spring 1993), 35–42; 'The Strange Disappearance of Civic America,' *American Prospect*, 24 (Winter 1996), 34–48; and 'Bowling Alone: America's Declining Social Capital,' *Journal of Democracy*, 6 (January 1995), 65–78. For a contrary view, see Robert W. Jackman and Ross A. Miller, 'Social Capital and Politics,' *Annual Review of Political Science*, 1 (1998), 47–73.
4. See, for example, 'A Nation of Spectators: How Civic Disengagement Weakens America and What We Can Do About It,' The Final Report of the Natural Commission on Civic Renewal, University of Maryland, 1999.
5. Alex P. Kellogg, 'Looking Inward, Freshmen Care Less About Politics and More About Money,' *Chronicle of Higher Education* (January 26, 2001), A47.
6. William A. Galston, 'Political Knowledge, Political Engagement, and Civic Education,' *Annual Review of Political* Science, 4 (2001), 219–220.
7. E.J. Dionne, Jr., *Why Americans Hate Politics* (New York: Touchstone, 1991), 332, 355.
8. Benjamin R. Barber, *A Passion for Democracy: American Essays* (Princeton, NJ: Princeton University Press, 1998), 97, 99.
9. Arthur M. Schlesinger, Jr., *The Cycles of American History* (Boston: Houghton Mifflin, 1986), 419.
10. Ibid., 430.
11. Quoted in James MacGregor Burns, *Leadership* (New York: Harper and Row, 1978), 148–49.
12. James Madison, Alexander Hamilton, and John Jay, *The Federalist Papers*, Madison, 'Number 57' (New York: Penguin Books [1788] 1987), 343.
13. Elshtain, *Democracy on Trial* (New York: Basic Books, 1995), 2.
14. Jonathan Rauch, *Demosclerosis: The Silent Killer of American Government* (New York: Times Books, 1994), 192.
15. Dick Morris, *The New Prince: Machiavelli Updated for the Twenty-First Century* (Los Angeles: Renaissance Books, 1999).
16. Richard Russo, *Nobody's Fool* (New York: Random House, 1993), 19.
17. Stephen Carter, *Civility: Manners, Morals, and the Etiquette of Democracy* (New York: Harper Perennial, 1998), 282.
18. Alan Wolfe, 'Make Nice, Not War,' *Wall Street Journal*, (April 28, 1998), A16.
19. John Danforth, 'What is the Point of Serving?,' excerpt from remarks on the Senate Floor, published in *Washington Post* (March 28, 1992), A20.

20. For an excellent historical discussion of this idea, see Albert O. Hirschman, *The Passions and the Interests: Political Arguments for Capitalism before Its Triumph* (Princeton, NJ: Princeton University Press, 1977).
21. Buzz Bissinger, *A Prayer for the City* (New York: Vintage Press, 1997), 293.
22. Ibid., 343.
23. The classic statement is found in Burns, *Leadership*. See especially Parts III and IV.

2. The Road to Public Reason

Public reason, trust, and the common good are the three pillars of con-temporary democratic leadership. They are equally important, but public reason is the best place to start because it directs our attention to the overall political context. When we hear commentary in the press about the decline in civility, or the divisive and polarized discourse in political campaigns, or the seeming inability of leaders to debate issues and policy rather than personality, or the inappropriateness of certain forms of argument in the public sphere, we are confronting the question of public reason. The challenge for contemporary democracies – and their citizens and leaders – is to shape disagreement and debate into collectively beneficial outcomes. The particular challenge for leaders is to understand their responsibilities and obligations in the midst of conflict.

'How is it possible for there to exist over time a just and stable society of free and equal citizens, who remain profoundly divided by reasonable religious, philosophical and moral doctrines?'[1] John Rawls's fundamental question is an apt formulation of the problem of contemporary democratic theory – and therefore an apt formulation of the leadership problem in modern democracies. One of the answers he provides is 'public reason,' a concept that requires us to explore such hefty issues as toleration, civility, and the conditions necessary for reasonable public deliberation in diverse, free societies. Can we achieve common ground or at least reasonable and just collective action through political engagement? To explore that question, we need to first set the foundation, a task which brings us back to the times of Machiavelli, then into the period of the American founding, and only then into our own. Machiavelli set the stage. Isaiah Berlin credits him with establishing this proposition: 'Men need rulers because they need someone to order human groups governed by diverse interests and bring them security, stability, and above all protection against enemies, to establish social institutions which alone enable men to satisfy needs and aspirations.'[2] We may not like some of Machiavelli's answers. Public reason may be a more palatable one. But whatever the response, modern politics accepts disorder and conflict as inevitable and leaders as an inevitable part of the response.

Machiavelli and da Vinci, or Why the Mona Lisa Helps Us Understand Politics

Look past the Mona Lisa smile (or smirk, depending on which interpretation you accept) to the background of the painting, the scene behind the figure of the mysterious woman. It is an unusual, almost surreal landscape. Rivers flow in twisted and violent patterns, cutting great gorges and winding around mountains and hills. Why da Vinci chose such a background is likely as much an enigma as Mona Lisa's expression. But thanks to the careful research of Roger Masters, we have some clues.[3] In the early 1500s, when da Vinci painted his famous portrait, rivers apparently were very much on his mind. He and Niccolo Machiavelli were engaged in an elaborate scheme to divert the waters of the Arno River. The two great Renaissance thinkers had found mutual cause in the defense of Florence, their beloved city-state. Surrounded by rival city-states and armies in the employ of the less than munificent Pope Alexander VI, Florentines were examining every possible means of protection. Raising their own army of citizen soldiers was one option. So was hiring mercenaries from France. So was the building of an elaborate defense. But those required money, and that meant taxes, and the fiscal condition of Florence, as well as the political climate, rendered those choices unappealing.

And so the two creative minds hatched their plot. To the west of Florence was Pisa, a city with a streak of independence and a longstanding mistrust, even hatred, of their eastern neighbors. But Pisa stood between Florence and the open sea, and flowing through Florence and into Pisa and eventually into the Ligurian Sea was the Arno River. Why not divert the Arno River in such a way that it bypassed Pisa and created a direct route to the sea for Florence? For da Vinci, the challenge of such a fantastical science and technology project was irresistible, and from his previous work with Milan he fully appreciated the practical uses for society of engineering. For Machiavelli, diplomat and public official *(The Prince* and other famous writings would come later), the strategic importance was uppermost in his mind. Advantage Florence by dis-advantaging Pisa. He was also in touch at the time with Agostino Vespucci, a relative of none other than the explorer Amerigo Vespucci, the explorer whose discovery of a distant land had convinced Florentines that emerging markets abroad held vast political and commercial value. To secure their own route to the sea and thus their future, Florence attempted an ambitious and far-flung engineering project centuries ahead of its time.

Predictably it failed. Just as da Vinci anticipated but could not develop the ability of man to create machines that would allow flight, so he anticipated the potential to change the landscape but could not himself achieve it on such a grand and ambitious scale. The engineer on site for the project incurred the wrath of da Vinci, and the artist, constantly in search of cash it seems, moved on to other adventures. Machiavelli's career suffered a setback. He was 'reassigned' but remained active in political affairs, raising a citizen's militia and advising on foreign affairs. Soderini, the ruler of Florence at the time, only added to his tarnished reputation as weak and indecisive. Having survived previous assassination plots and less violent attempts to remove him, his power continued its downward trajectory. In a few short years he would lose it all and provide Machiavelli with a model of what a prince should not be.

As Masters so cleverly details, the unsuccessful collaboration between Machiavelli and da Vinci was more than a minor historical footnote. It illuminates much about the thinking of the times – and so much about the intellectual legacy handed down from Machiavelli, and therefore so much of the thinking of our own times. Machiavelli laid the foundation for our current perspective on leadership. Understanding his legacy depends first on understanding the context in which he was writing. The creativity sparked by the Renaissance notwithstanding, it was an anxious and unsettling time. In Italy, city-states were indeed rivals. The Church in Rome and the ruling Popes were corrupt by any definition of the term. Every region was either on the attack or being attacked. Throughout Europe the situation was no better. Philippe de Commines, a French diplomat of the times, wrote to Charles VIII of France, explaining his assessment of the current state of affairs: 'God has not made any created being in this world, neither man nor beast, nor anything else, but he has set up something in opposition to it ... France has England as a check, England has Scotland, and Spain, Portugal.' He went on to describe the similar state of hostility among the German and Italian states. Strife was judged to be a permanent condition 'all the world over.'[4]

Machiavelli – strategist, patriot of Florence, public official, skeptic of doctrinaire religion, and now discreet critic of the feeble Soderini – began to see leadership in a light different from the philosophers of ancient Greek and Roman times. They wrote without reference to the struggles of politics and therefore of matters far removed from what Machiavelli observed. Their musings provided no guidance for him or the rulers he served. Years after the failed Arno River project, he crafted *The Prince*.

> I may be held presumptuous ... But since my intent is to write something useful to whoever understands it, it has appeared to me more fitting to go to the effectual truth of the thing than to the imagination of it. And many have imagined republics and principalities that have never been seen or known to exist in truth; for it is so far from how one lives to how one should live that he who lets go of what is done for what should be done learns his ruin rather than his preservation.[5]

The Prince remains 'useful' to this day but for reasons far more complex than its reputation suggests. It is essential to highlight this one main contribution: Machiavelli firmly believed that societies control their destiny. To be sure, luck or fortune plays some part, but we are not without resources. In fact, we have little option but to act, and a critical factor, an indispensable factor in taking charge of our future is strong leadership. No doubt recalling at least a little his ill-fated collaboration with da Vinci, he wrote metaphorically:

> ... that fortune is arbiter of half our actions, but also that she leaves the other half or close to it, for us to govern. And I liken her to one of those violent rivers which, when they become enraged, flood the plains, ruin the trees and the buildings, lift earth from this part, drop in another; each person flees before them, everyone yields to their impetus without being able to hinder them in every regard. And although they are like this, it is not as if men, when times are quiet, could not provide for them with dikes and dams so that when they rise later, either they go by a canal or their impetus is neither so wanton nor so damaging. It happens similarly with fortune, which shows her power where virtue has not been put in order to resist her and therefore turns her impetus where she knows that dams and dikes have not been made to contain her. And if you consider Italy, which is the seat of these variations and that which has given them motion, you will see a country without dams and without any dike.[6]

Machiavelli set the terms for our contemporary discussions of leadership. Disorder and conflict are inherent in the modern world. But we are not powerless, passive victims of the raging rivers. The task of politics and therefore the tasks of political leaders is to manage that conflict. To be sure, we have to examine critically some of Machiavelli's suggestions for achieving those objectives, but the basic dilemma is clear. Providing stability requires the use of power – occasionally, maybe even often. The use of power requires skills and tasks not always in harmony with some other priorities, such as freedom, compassion and altruism, to mention just a few.

That is why Machiavelli was subversive then and still unsettling today. If everyone were virtuous, the leader could also be virtuous. But in a 'world (that) consists only of the vulgar'[7] and where people are 'ungrateful, voluble, anxious to avoid danger, and covetous of gain'[8] a leader would actually be *more* merciful if he learned 'not to be good' – for goodness, in that classic sense of the term, would paradoxically 'injure the whole community' by allowing disorder and conflict. According to Isaiah Berlin, Machiavelli was:

> ... convinced that what are commonly thought of as the central Christian virtues, whatever their intrinsic value, are insuperable obstacles to the building of the kind of society that he wishes to see; a society which, moreover, he assumes that it is natural for all men to want – the kind of community that, in his view, satisfies men's permanent desires and interests.[9]

How do we achieve one set of goals without jeopardizing another set? How do we provide order within constraints of ethics and justice? I will argue that 'public reason' – the capacity to disagree reasonably and fairly while formulating and pursuing political ends – is one modern answer, but first we need to examine another episode on the way to our present day.

Hamilton's Dilemma

It would be convenient for our analysis if Alexander Hamilton's essays in the celebrated *Federalist Papers* had footnoted Machiavelli, or if historians had been able to unearth copies of *The Prince* or *The Discourses* among his papers. But the history of the influence of certain ideas is usually never that obvious. Scholars have in fact traced strands from Machiavelli to Montesquieu and then to the Enlightenment thinkers, such as Locke and Smith, and then directly into the writings of the founders. But those strands take some convoluted twists and turns. There is not a straight, linear connection between the Italian thinker and one of the authors of the Constitution. For our immediate purpose, however, we need only observe some common sentiments, a kind of parallel analysis that yielded some different conclusions about government while sharing some critically important premises.

Recall Machiavelli's claim that we affect our destiny and consider Hamilton's declaration in the very first paragraph of the very first *Federalist Paper*. Though he had not schemed with a colonial da Vinci in a grandiose engineering project, he did believe:

> ... that it seems to be reserved to the people of this country, by their conduct and example, to decide the important question, whether societies of men are really capable or not of establishing good government from reflection and choice, or whether they are forever destined to depend for their political constitutions on accident and force. If there be any truth in the remark, the crisis at which we are arrived may with propriety be regarded as the era in which that decision is to be made; and a wrong election of the part we shall act may, in this view, deserve to be considered as the general misfortune of mankind.[10]

On the one hand, *The Federalist Papers* were merely a series of op-ed pieces addressed to the voters of New York to generate support for the Constitution. On the other hand, they command our attention today for their careful analysis of the challenge faced by democratic governments everywhere. The stakes were high. At this time and place, Machiavelli's proposition would be put to its clearest test. The 85 essays – 51 by Hamilton; 26 by James Madison; five by John Jay; and three jointly by Madison and Hamilton – describe the proposed constitution, but they also constitute a nuanced philosophical argument for various processes of government – a declaration that citizens and their leaders, despite their inherent conflictual natures, can achieve just collective action.

They also are a polemic, an argument against the existing *Articles of Confederation*. It was, in fact, the Articles that formed the backdrop for Hamilton's primary argument, and in a manner similar to the way in which the fragmented city-states of Italy formed the backdrop for Machiavelli. The *Articles* provided no unity among the states of the newly formed country. The government consequently was 'destitute of energy.'[11] Mere tinkering to change the 'material defects in our national system' was inadequate. The problems 'do not proceed from minute or partial imperfections, but from fundamental errors in the structure of the building.' Defenders of the *Articles* and critics of the Constitution 'seem to cherish with blind devotion the political monster of an imperium in imperio ... Each State yielding to the persuasive voice of immediate interest or convenience has successively withdrawn its support, till the frail and tottering edifice seems to fall upon our heads and to crush us beneath its ruins.'[12] For proof of the inability of the government to ensure tranquility, the conveners of the Constitution pointed to Shay's rebellion in Vermont – the conflagration caused by debtors who rejected the powers of the national government.

Instability was in the air. The individual states were spinning away from the center driven by 'love of power' disguised rhetorically as a love of liberty. Hamilton was not an engineer nor did he have a da Vinci at his side, but it seems that he intuitively grasped the laws of physics.

> From this spirit it happens that in every political association which is formed upon the principle of uniting in a common interest a number of lesser sovereignties, there will be found a kind of eccentric tendency in the subordinate or inferior orbs by the operation of which there will be a perpetual tendency to fly off from the common center.[13]

Power of one kind had to check power of another kind. The answer was not diminished power but a countervailing one. Stability comes from balancing centrifugal and centripetal forces.

While all three contributors to *The Federalist Papers* make the case for a strengthened national government, Hamilton's voice is the most forceful and it finds its clearest expression in his arguments for establishing a presidency. 'A feeble executive implies a feeble execution of government.' The office needs 'energy,' 'vigor,' 'expedition,' and 'competent powers.' Hamilton's case was an implicit critique of the states' tendency to devise governmental structures in which the legislature was supreme. Legislatures are 'best adapted to deliberation and wisdom,' he wrote, 'and best calculated to conciliate the confidence of the people and to secure their privileges and interests.' But an orderly polity also requires 'personal firmness' and 'stability of the system of administration.' He declared '... [L]et us make a firm stand for our safety, our tranquility, our dignity, our reputation. Let us at last break the fatal charm which has too long seduced us from the paths felicity and prosperity.'[14]

The 'fatal charm' to which Hamilton refers suggests that in his view societies can be misled into thinking that liberty without restraint was some aspirational ideal. Too much power was a problem; but so too was unrestrained liberty. Madison put the matter in these terms: '... [L]iberty may be endangered by the abuses of liberty as well as by the abuses of power; that there are numerous instances of the former as well as of the latter; and that the former, rather than the latter, is apparently most to be apprehended by the United States.'[15] The authors of *The Federalist Papers* were in no way abandoning the project of liberty. But, as Isaac Kramnick describes it, they were seeking to reassert the 'politics of energy' during a time when the 'politics of liberty' dominated political discourse.[16] The task is to devise 'some institution that blends stability with liberty.'[17]   The dilemma for Hamilton – and Madison and Jay – was not that the establishment of order necessarily meant the loss of liberty. On the contrary, a properly constructed order was a better provider of liberty. In the now familiar words that found their way into the preamble of the Constitution, their project was to 'form a more perfect union, establish justice, insure domestic tranquility, provide for the common defense, promote the general welfare, and secure the blessings of liberty to ourselves and our posterity.'[18]

It is at this point, however, that we need to recognize an important element in the case made in *The Federalist Papers* – important in advancing us to the concept of public reason and the view of leadership associated with it. The proponents of the Constitution, the Federalists, did indeed wish to centralize government, or at least make it more central than the structure created by *The Articles of Confederation*. Their critics, the Anti-Federalists, were concerned that the proposed Constitution would diminish the voice of the people. For example, rather than the vibrant, responsive state legislatures – local and directly in touch with the electors – the proposed Congress would be distant, large, and made up of an aristocratic elite. The Anti-Federalists believed that the local legislatures could reflect the will of the people more accurately because the elected would be more like the electors. As one opponent of the Constitution wrote, representatives 'should be a true picture of the people; possess the knowledge of their circumstances and their wants; sympathize in all their distresses; and be disposed to seek their true interests.' Representatives need not be, nor should they be, men of 'brilliant talents.' There should be instead a 'sameness, as to residence and interests, between the representative and his constituents.'[19] In the view of the Anti-Federalists, they should mirror the preferences of the citizens they represent, perfectly reflecting their vices and virtues, ambitions and interests, their needs and their wants:

Representatives should have the same views and interests with the people at large. They should think, feel, and act like them and in fine should be an exact miniature of their constituents. They should be (if we may use the expression) the whole body politic, with all its property, rights and privileges reduced to a smaller scale, every part being diminished just in proportion.[20]

Hamilton, Madison, and Jay had a different metaphor in mind – not a mirror but a filter. Their argument is intricate and draws from a set of propositions underlying political discourse at that time. Individuals were considered creatures of interests and passions. Those interests arose from and were given definition by a curious combination of reason, which enabled individuals to recognize and calculate their interests, and self-love which transformed their calculation of interest into self-interest. To advance one's interests, a citizen would join with like-minded allies and form factions. Those factions would compete and (as Madison famously wrote in Federalist Paper Number 10) *the* problem for government was resolving those conflicting claims, reconciling competition, and ensuring some sense of order and justice – while at the same time respecting not only the *need* for liberty but also the *inevitability* of individuals asserting their autonomy. To simply mirror those factional disputes among the citizenry was an invitation to chaos. To simply transfer the passionate self-interested debates into the structure of government was to enfeeble the institutions rather than strengthen them. Representatives should 'refine and enlarge' public opinion so as to 'discern the true interest of the people.'[21] That, for Madison, was one of the primary differences between a republic, which he favored, and a democracy.

David Weaver makes the case well by suggesting that the authors of *The Federalist Papers* were, in effect, balancing a realistic appraisal of the basic factious nature of citizens and leaders with an aspiration to achieve a true public interest. As he put it, '... [A] central problem of governance and, perforce, of leadership would be to guide and control the irrational aspects of human nature while striving to promote and develop the rational.'[22] Leaders had responsibility for shaping the tone and the nature of public debate. They could make it rational by invoking reason or they could merely echo the passionate, self-interested claims of their constituents.

The filter argument remains contested even to this day in part because it depends on other propositions – two in particular – which are also contested. One is that leaders, once in government, can display those qualities or virtues that enable them to debate and thereby discover the public interest. The other is that the institutional design – the structures of the institution and the procedures – should create incentives for capable individuals to enter government, provide rewards for them to act in that manner and create a selection process that identifies and recruits the most talented. For the filter argument to have any credence both those contingencies are necessary; neither is sufficient.

Leaders must not only possess certain qualities of mind and heart; they must also be placed in institutional structures that cultivate those qualities and reward those individuals who manifest them.

Whether the case of Madison, Hamilton, and Jay is disproved by current events is an intriguing question. In today's political scene, there are certainly some observers who believe that the most capable leaders in society are those least attracted to public office. But there is no doubt that the Founders were convinced of the soundness of their brief. One of the strongest arguments for the constitution, in their view, was that the structure made it possible, indeed probable, that the citizens most capable of leadership would find public service an attractive proposition. Even more to the point, the constitutional forms would function so that the traits most desirable in leaders would be the same traits that enabled aspirants to public office to navigate the selection system successfully. There were no guarantees, of course: 'enlightened statesmen would not always be at the helm,' and 'experience has taught mankind the necessity of auxiliary precautions,' which is why trust alone would not prevent the abuse of power.[23] Still, the Founders wanted to raise the odds as high as they could. Jay, for example, argued that the extensiveness of the republic created a larger pool of talent:

> When once an efficient national government is established, the best men in the country will not only consent to serve, but also will be appointed to manage it; for, although town or country, or other contracted influence, may place men in state assemblies, or senates, or courts of justice, or executive departments, yet more general and extensive reputation for talents and other qualifications will be necessary to recommend men to offices under the national government – especially as it will have the widest field for choice, and never experience that want of proper persons which is not uncommon in some of the States. Hence, it will result that the administration, the political counsels, and the judicial decisions of the national government will be more wise, systematical, and judicious than those of individual states.[24]

And in another section:

> ... the President and senators so chosen will always be the number of those who best understand our national interests ... who are best able to promote those interests, and whose reputation for integrity inspires and merits confidence.[25]

Hamilton supplied a similar analysis. In *The Federalist Papers*, number 35, after presenting his own version of the filter argument, he argues that representatives will go to great efforts to understand the need of their constituents and establish 'strong cords of sympathy' with them – although they will avoid the 'momentary humors or dispositions' of the populace.[26] They will, that is, come to understand the general habits and interest of the people, not their fleeting passions. Political leaders wise enough to make those distinctions can be found among all classes and all walks of life. One of the functions of the constitutional system is to ferret them out, to provide the means and opportunities for them to be identified and enticed into public service.

The story so far brings us to this point. Conflict is inevitable in diverse societies. In order to bring stability to the conflict and to ensure that people of different beliefs and interests can live together, leaders are necessary. But those leaders must possess a set of qualities and talents that allow them to participate in and manage a process that extracts from the citizens their 'true interests.' Machiavelli himself reveals a tendency to this view more forcefully in another of his works, *Discourses on Livy*:

> But as to prudence and stability, I say that a people is more prudent, more stable, and of better judgment than a prince. Not without cause may the voice of a people be likened to that of God; for one sees a universal opinion produce marvelous effects in its forecasts, so that it appears to foresee its ill and its good by a hidden virtue. As to judging things, if a people hears two orators who incline to different sides, when they are of equal value, very few times does one see it not take up the better opinion and not persuaded of the truth that it hears.[27]

The role of leaders in democratic societies is to create conditions that enable the 'true wisdom' of the people to emerge, and for all the insight provided by Hamilton, Madison, and Jay, the specific qualities leaders need to fulfill this responsibility remain ill-defined. Civility matters, to be sure, and not only a tolerance for opposing views but a recognition that other views might improve a strongly held preconceived opinion. A willingness to publicly and honestly defend a point of view, exposing it to criticism and debate, is another requisite for political debate to achieve the standard of public reason. In other words, discerning the true wisdom of the people requires wisdom of a different sort from the leader. The authors of *The Federalist Papers* were merely laying the groundwork for others to follow.

John Rawls and Public Reason

We leap ahead to the present era, past the tectonic social changes caused by industrialization and technological advances, through the periods of intense and tragic international conflict, and into a political climate where, as Jean Bethke Elshtain sees it, 'democracy is on trial.'[28] Rates of political participation have declined, as measured by voting, work on campaigns, or simple awareness of key political issues. Commentators typically decry the low level of trust in public officials and government institutions. The coarsening of public debate, marked not only by negative campaigns but also legal and ethical prosecution of political opponents, seems to have crossed some problematic threshold.[29] Eric M. Uslaner's study of Congress led him to conclude, 'American society and its politics have hardened ... Politics is now not just a serious business but a highly polarized one. Give and take has given way to non-negotiable demands .... Confrontation, not dialogue, dominates ...'[30] Indeed, the very purpose of politics appears to have degenerated in most people's eyes to the single-minded pursuit of their own particular interests. Americans hate politics, in the opinion of E.J. Dionne, because we have lost all sense of 'the public good.' Over the last thirty years of political polarization, politics has stopped being a deliberative process through which people resolved disputes, found remedies and moved forward.'[31] Cappella and Jamieson implicate the media for the 'spiral of cynicism' they reinforce: the acts of politicians are explained solely as strategic moves to enhance their electability.[32] When Bill Bradley quit the Senate a few years ago, he declared, 'Politics is broken ... Neither political party speaks to people where they live their lives.'[33]

This is not what Hamilton, Madison, and Jay had in mind. Despite their realism and grounded analysis, their aspirations for political discourse were higher.

Of course, a lot happened since the Renaissance and the Founding. Modernity intervened, with all its attendant costs and benefits. Society fragmented into specialized spheres: education became distinct from parenting; church and state no longer perfectly overlapped; law and morality branched off from each other. Interactions among people became purposive or functional; we come together for commercial transactions or to fulfill other interests and needs. A host of legal mechanisms arose: contracts, organizations, and bureaucracy, leading to what is generally called 'rational coordination.'

Modernity did have its advantages. It brought efficiency to a more complex society. It also brought toleration and enabled free and diverse peoples to live together in a manner that diffused at least somewhat the potential for conflict. But, as Selznik points out, it came with a price. 'The fundamental truth,' he writes, 'is that modernity weakens culture and fragments experience. The gains of modernity are won, not easily and smoothly, but at a significant cost to the harmony and stability of human experience.'[34]

It is against this backdrop of profound sociological change and concern over its impact on democratic prospects that John Rawls presents the concept of public reason. He is perhaps the most influential contemporary political philosopher, not necessarily because of his persuasiveness or eloquence – indeed his views are controversial and his writing dense and abstract – but rather because of the intricacy and meticulousness of his overall theory, the way the pieces fit together so tightly to form a coherent package. *Theory of Justice* changed the agenda of liberal thought by introducing a compelling argument for egalitarianism within liberty.[35] *Political Liberalism*, a different kind of work, has also spawned a wealth of commentary.[36] In this second work especially, Rawls weaves together a set of ideas and concepts that serve as the ground rules for political discourse in a pluralistic society where people differ profoundly in their beliefs and principles. What are the terms of engagement? What are the benchmarks against which we can measure the current political climate? One is public reason. We need to examine it in a way that does justice to Rawls' claims while also framing it so that we can examine its implications for leadership theory. Is public reason attainable and, if so, desirable? And if it is attainable and desirable, what does it require of leaders?

Public reason, according to Rawls, is the way we should disagree on fundamental political questions, given that disagreement is inevitable and permanent in societies of free and equal citizens. 'In a democratic society,' he writes, 'public reason is the reason of equal citizens who, as a collective body, exercise final political and coercive powers over one another in enacting laws and amending their constitution.'[37] If the citizenry calls upon the state to coerce other citizens through laws, and thereby limits the freedom of citizens in the name of a collective good or order, the decision must be arrived at legitimately. One criterion for legitimacy is whether the reasons for the action were publicly explained and understood by those affected, even if some remain opposed. The stakes are high. Public reason becomes one of the fundamental obligations of citizens, a defining characteristic of citizenship:

> [Citizens] should be ready to explain the basis of their actions to one another in terms each could reasonably expect that others might endorse as consistent with their freedom and equality. Trying to meet this condition is one of the tasks that this ideal of democratic politics asks of us. Understanding how to conduct oneself as a democratic citizen includes understanding an ideal of public reason.[38]

And:

> What public reason asks is that citizens be able to explain their vote to one another in terms of a reasonable balance of public political values.[39]

Public reason, though it imposes extremely high standards on democratic discourse, is a desirable standard for democratic deliberation because it respects the profound differences among citizens (indeed, it embraces them) while recognizing as well our interdependence and need to work with those who do differ from us. As demanding as it is on citizens, however, it is even more so on leaders, to the point that we are led to a critical departure, indeed inversion of sorts, of Machiavelli's view of the world. Whereas Machiavelli's response to the 'vulgarity' and avariciousness of the citizenry was to ask leaders to reflect those vices to an even greater degree, Rawls's stake in public reason leads him in an opposite direction. Leaders are obligated not to embody the differences of their constituents nor to mimic their vices but rather to transcend them. Closer to the sentiments of *The Federalist Papers*, Rawls endorses a kind of filter approach, a hope that the process can control and guide the irrational while promoting the rational. Discourse in the public arena, or even politics in general, is unavoidably messy and harsh; nevertheless, citizens should aspire to reasoned debate. While remaining free and open, deliberation must be restrained by an awareness of what is possible and permissible to achieve in the political realm and how those arguments need to be presented.

Arguing for 'restraint' is not a comfortable posture for those with liberal instincts; and Rawls is extremely careful about how that restraint takes force. It comes about not through legal structures but rather through the incentives fashioned through institutional design and also through a dependence on a leader's virtue and sense of duty. It is a moral not a legal imperative.[40] Contrary to the charges leveled by his critics, Rawls relies heavily on virtue to achieve his liberal ends. For public reason to work, citizens must fulfill an ethical duty; leaders even more so.

Implicitly, Rawls therefore enters into a classic divide in the leadership literature: can we construct a theory of leadership on the hopeful premise that leaders are capable of acting out of a sense of duty and in a manner that potentially works against immediate interest? Indeed, are they not obligated to do so? A negative response is an implicit rejection of public reason as a guidepost. A positive response, though not automatically an embrace of public reason, at least admits its possibility.

Public reason is a deceptively difficult standard to achieve. It presents a paradox. On the one hand, public reason limits discourse because it sets ground rules on what are or are not legitimate public arguments. On the other hand, it elevates public discourse by providing a rigorous standard. By understanding the paradox, and the charges leveled against each aspect of it, we can begin to fashion an understanding of the obligations of leaders, if public reason is to accomplish what Rawls intends.

The Paradox of Public Reason: Aspiration and Limitation

In Rawls's world, deliberation is not a free-for-all in which all kinds of justifications for positions are legitimate. Merely expressing an opinion is undemanding. Justifying, explaining, and defending an action in terms others can understand and in terms consistent with what we mean by freedom and equality is a higher standard. Certain claims, such as appeals to religious traditions or 'comprehensive beliefs,' fall within the parameters of public reason only when some very particular conditions apply. For example, opinion expressed in terms that make sense only to the citizens expressing them is mere discourse, not reason or at least not public reason. Politics is not, in other words, the venue for discovering truth – a worthy and desirable undertaking to be sure but one that becomes potentially dangerous when aligned with the coercive potential of state action. The justifications that legitimately support political action must have different features from arguments acceptable in non-political institutions, such as the church, family, and associations. Membership in those social units is voluntary, or if it is not fully voluntary there is at least an exit option more possible than leaving the political unit. Therefore, those who disagree with the argument may withdraw, an alternative not available to a citizen of a state. In a democracy, there is no feasible alternative to living with others of differing political views. Moreover, the state has the coercive power to impose a collective decision on those who disagree with the decision. Because of the unique impacts of political decisions and the unique powers of the state, political debate is fundamentally different – or it should be – from debate and disagreement in other non-political and private contexts.

To put it another way, not all matters need to be brought into the political arena. Not all disputes are political. There are limits to what can be and should be achieved in politics, and the arguments for political action cannot legitimately draw upon personal, which is to say non-political, reasons understood only by the individual articulating the claim.

The criticisms of such a position are not surprising, for Rawls does present a rather simplified psychology of how individuals form their beliefs and translate them into political opinions. Undoubtedly, political positions represent a complex convergence of influences upon an individual. To separate a particular thread from a densely woven fabric is difficult. Even if it could be done, the entire tapestry would unravel. Or to use Michael Sandel's imagery, it is impossible to 'bracket' certain fundamental beliefs or principles, to set them aside and not have recourse to them when we make our public arguments.[41]

The critics have had their influence, forcing Rawls and other liberals to explain carefully their strictures on public discourse. In a carefully developed section of *Political Liberalism*, Rawls goes to great lengths to describe an 'inclusive' and an 'exclusive' view. The exclusive view is the one critics would surely reject. It relies upon a bright line distinction between 'comprehensive beliefs' and those beliefs citizens might legitimately call upon in the public arena. The former are strictly excluded because they depend upon justifications, such as a particular religious tradition, that not all citizens can comprehend or accept.

The inclusive view dims the bright line. It would allow citizens 'to present what they regard as the basis of political values rooted in their comprehensive doctrines, provided they do this in ways that strengthen the idea of public reason itself.'[42] Rawls comes close to making a circular argument. Apparently the only way we know if a statement is publicly reasonable is by determining whether it leads to public reason. But Rawls provides an illustration. He points to Martin Luther King, Jr., as a prime example of someone crafting a clearly moral, yet political, argument based in good part on a religious tradition. Now, King did construct the moral case so that it matched well the fundamental political values of the society. His skill was an ability to move from a moral and religious tradition to the principles and values inherent in a society that endorsed a Declaration of Independence. As Rawls explains, 'Religious doctrines clearly underlie King's view and are important in his appeals. Yet they are expressed in general terms; and they fully support constitutional values and accord with public reason.'[43]

Rawls's adoption of the inclusive view is a concession. Even with that concession, his limitations on what can enter public debate still seem too severe to some critics and too artificial given the reality of how people form their political positions and explain them to others. He does indeed wish to impose a filter to screen out certain arguments in the public sphere. His stance, however, is consistent with the tradition of 'liberalism of fear' – the strand of liberal thought, well-articulated by Judith Shklar. She worried about 'ideologies of solidarity' (similar to Rawls's worry about comprehensive beliefs) and their potential for oppression when merged with politics. Like Rawls, she emphatically defends a boundary between the personal and the political. She would concede that the boundary is provisional and constantly contested. She would agree that citizens might dispute the location of the boundary, and that some will favor a larger political sphere as beneficial to society whereas others will prefer it to be smaller. And she would acknowledge that conflict is permanent in diverse societies.[44] But to place all conflict – religious, familial, associational – in the public sphere is to impossibly burden political institutions and to risk outcomes of the most frightening sort. A 'liberalism of fear' would not submit (indeed debase) all value disagreements, whatever their origins, to the vicissitudes of political contests.

That is not to dismiss the significance of deeply-held beliefs, religious or otherwise. 'To seek emotional and personal development in the bosom of a community or in romantic self-expression is a choice open to citizens in liberal societies,' Shklar wrote. But those are 'apolitical impulses ... which distract us from the main task of politics when presented as political doctrines.'[45] 'Public reason,' which steers public discourse away from appeals to personal belief, does not delegitimize those beliefs. But it does recognize the danger of basing political actions on rationales not understood by those who must live under laws derived from such rationales. In this respect, Rawls's public reason is unquestionably a defensive posture, a limitation on political society, and one akin to Shklar's analysis of fear as a primary reason for a liberal brand of politics.

On the other hand – and this is why it is a paradox – public reason is also an aspiration, for it seeks to elevate public discourse. At the same time that it is motivated by a 'fear' of what may happen in the political realm, it sets a standard for the quality of public debate. A justification must be understandable to others who disagree, not because it may result in agreement and not only for strategic reasons of persuading others to align with one's position, but out of respect for the beliefs of others. Mutual respect is a step beyond toleration.[46] It requires a recognition of the moral standing of others and a willingness to engage and deliberate with those who hold very different moral frameworks. It does not require accepting the others' beliefs. But it does require (to use Gutmann and Thompson's felicitous term) an 'economy of moral disagreement,' an attempt to limit the disagreement to the fewest sources of disputes.[47] The consequence is that understanding and persuasion supplant bargaining as the goal of political discourse. Deliberation aspires to more than simply the pursuit of private interest. It rises above a mere contest for position and power.[48] Yet it stops well short of the pursuit of the full truth.

Later, I will return to these points raised by Rawls and Gutmann and Thompson. For now, we can conclude that public reason obligates citizens to adopt a disposition and a set of democratic virtues. It is normative, principled, and moral. In Rawls's words:

> The virtues of political cooperation that make a constitutional regime possible are, then, very great virtues. I mean, for example, the virtues of tolerance and being ready to meet others halfway, and the virtue of reasonableness and the sense of fairness. When these virtues are widespread in a society and sustain its political conception of justice, they constitute a very great public good, part of society's political capital.[49]

A Preliminary Conclusion

The portrait of liberal leadership sketched so far is surely incomplete, but several essential characteristics have emerged. Machiavelli's reputation for ruthlessness is not wholly undeserved, although his obsession with restoring order in the midst of conflict is understandable given the times in which he lived. But in the midst of his treatise are insights which are very much applicable to these times. Societies are diverse; politics arises from disagreement and conflict; the object of government is to resolve that conflict, and leaders are at the center of that enterprise. When Machiavelli writes that leaders would actually be more merciful if they 'learned not to be good,' he does indeed give us reason for concern. And of course that conclusion is based on a less than lofty version of human nature. If leaders followed the rules of goodness, if they did only what they ought to do, the general 'vulgarity' of mankind would determine the fate of society in ways not very pleasant. The larger message, though, is that society need not surrender to that fate. Leaders are responsible for 'building those dams and dikes' to divert the waters to more advantageous directions, and that obligation requires a set of skills and virtues different from what we conventionally think of as virtues.

Hamilton and his fellow essayists, Madison and Jay, move farther along the path, presenting a more hopeful portrait of the possibilities of collective action. They certainly saw the same danger in disorder as Machiavelli did, but whereas the Florentine defined the public good almost solely as the absence of the 'public bad,' the authors of *The Federalist Papers* had positive aspects in mind as well. That 'true interest' of the people could only be discerned, however, through reason and deliberation – political activities which again fall to leaders to manage and which again require a certain set of skills and virtues.

Rawls goes even further. Though he devotes almost none of his treatise to an explicit consideration of leadership, the implication is clear. If reasoned deliberation is essential for liberal society and if understanding those with whom we disagree is essential for a fair and just society, the obligation of leaders becomes considerable. Rather than succumbing to the 'vulgar' nature of citizens, leaders must bring out their capacity for tolerance and rational discourse. It is a demanding role. It, too, requires a particular set of virtues and skills. That set has yet to be firmly identified, but it includes the ability to engender trust among citizens; and trust rests on the perception that leaders are pursuing a public good rather than their own self-interest. Exploring those propositions is the object of the rest of this inquiry.

Notes

1. John Rawls, *Political Liberalism* (New York: Columbia University Press, 1996), 4.
2. Isaiah Berlin, 'The Originality of Machiavelli,' in I. Berlin, *The Proper Study of Mankind: An Anthology of Essays* (New York: Farrar, Straus and Giroux, 1998), 284.
3. The account draws directly from Roger D. Masters, *Fortune Is a River: Leonardo da Vinci and Niccolo Machiavelli's Magnificent Dream to Change the Course of Florentine History* (New York: Penguin Putnam, 1999).
4. Quoted in John Hale, *The Civilization of Europe in the Renaissance* (New York: Atheneum, 1994), 94.
5. Niccolo Machiavelli, *The Prince*, trans. Harvey C. Mansfield, Jr. (Chicago: University of Chicago Press, [1532] 1985), 61.
6. Ibid., 98.
7. Ibid., 71.
8. Ibid., 66.
9. Berlin, 290.
10. James Madison, Alexander Hamilton, and John Jay, *The Federalist Papers*, Hamilton, 'Number 1' (New York: Penguin Books, [1788] 1987), 87.
11. Madison et al., *The Federalist Papers*, Hamilton, 'Number 15,' 147.
12. Ibid., 147, 151.
13. Ibid., 150
14. Ibid., 147.

15. Madison et al., *The Federalist Papers*, Madison, 'Number 63,' 373.
16. Madison et al., *The Federalist Papers*, Kramnick, 'Introduction,' viz. 16–28.
17. Madison et al., *The Federalist Papers*, Madison, 'Number 63,' 371.
18. U.S. Constitution, Preamble.
19. Quoted in Herbert J. Storing, *What the Anti-Federalists Were For: The Political Thought of The Opponents of the Constitution* (Chicago: University of Chicago Press, 1981), 17.
20. Quoted in Madison et al., *The Federalist Papers*, Kramnick, 'Introduction,' 44. Kramnick develops the mirror-versus-filter metaphors in some detail.
21. Madison et al., *The Federalist Papers*, Madison, 'Number 10,' 126.
22. David Weaver, 'Leadership, Locke, and the Federalist,' *American Journal of Political Science*, 41, 2 (April 1997), 425.
23. Madison et al., *The Federalist Papers*, Madison, 'Number 51,' 320.
24. Madison et al., *The Federalist Papers*, Jay, 'Number 3,' 95.
25. Madison et al., *The Federalist Papers*, Hamilton, 'Number 36,' 235.
26. Ibid.
27. Niccolo Machiavelli, *Discourses on Livy*, trans. Harvey C. Mansfield and Nathan Tarcov (Chicago: University of Chicago Press, 1996), 117–118.
28. Jean Bethke Elshtain, *Democracy on Trial* (New York: Basic Books, 1995).
29. Benjamin Ginsberg and Martin Shefter, *Politics by Other Means: Politicians, Prosecutors and the Press from Watergate to Whitewater* (New York: Norton Books, 1999).
30. Eric M. Uslaner, *The Decline of Comity in Congress* (Ann Arbor: University of Michigan Press, 1993), 1–2. See also Kathleen Hall Jamieson, *Civility in the House of Representatives: The 105th Congress* (Philadelphia: Annenberg Public Policy Center, 1999).
31. E.J. Dionne, Jr., *Why Americans Hate Politics* (New York: Touchstone Books, 1991), 332.
32. Joseph N. Cappella and Kathleen Hall Jamieson, *Spiral of Cynicism: The Press and the Public Good* (New York: Oxford University Press, 1997).
33. Quoted in Paul Starobin, 'The Bradley Question,' *National Journal*, 31 (August 21, 1999).
34. Philip Selznick, *The Moral Commonwealth: Social Theory and the Promise of Community* (Berkeley: University of California Press, 1994), 8.
35. John Rawls, *A Theory of Justice* (Cambridge, MA: Belknap Press, 1971).
36. John Rawls, *Political Liberalism*.
37. Ibid., 214.
38. Ibid., 218.
39. Ibid., 243.
40. Ibid., 217.
41. Michael J. Sandel, *Democracy's Discontent: America in Search of a Public Philosophy* (Cambridge, MA: Belknap Press, 1996).
42. John Rawls, *Political Liberalism*, 247.
43. Ibid., 250.
44. Judith N. Shklar, 'The Liberalism of Fear,' in Stanley Hoffmann, ed., *Political Thought and Political Thinkers* (Chicago: University of Chicago Press, 1998), 3–20.
45. Ibid., 18.
46. Amy Gutmann and Dennis Thompson, *Democracy and Disagreement: Why Moral Conflict Cannot Be Avoided in Politics, and What Should Be Done about It* (Cambridge, MA: Belknap Press, 1996), 80.
47. Ibid., 85.
48. John Rawls, *Political Liberalism*, 239.
49. Ibid., 157.

3. Locke's Prerogative, Jay's Pirouette: Why Trust Still Matters in Contemporary Democratic Leadership

Trust is the second of three pillars in democratic leadership. The recent declines of trust in modern society have received the attention of a number of scholars as well as commentators in the popular press, but little attention has been paid to the fundamental reasons why trust matters in a democracy. In fact, democratic theory is far better at explaining why mistrust is more prudent and advisable. In a theory of government built on mistrust, why do we worry about declining in trust in leaders?

Prelude

In July 2000, Jack Welch, the chairman of General Electric and the management icon of the moment, received a record-breaking $7.1 million advance for his proposed book. Journalists were quick to explain the contract as the publisher's attempt to replicate the success of Lee Iaccoca's bestseller of the previous decade. Business had a good run in the 1990s. General Electric was one of the most admired enterprises, at least among large, established companies, and Welch's guidance was presumably one of the factors. Predictably, Welch was asked his view on a range of topics, but when it came to politics he demurred. 'I don't touch politics,' he said. The reason:

> In government, the best ideas don't always win. The president has to deal with Congress. In government, you're always compromising. You sell out on some principle and get something else for it. In business you're not. You can be totally free. In a company, we have the luxury of being able to remove values we don't like.[1]

Welch's analysis suffers from oversimplification. And his choice of words – 'selling out on principle' – reveals the usual perception among businessmen of the seamier side of public life. Yet he has stumbled into an important insight about political leadership. In a pluralistic society that places a high priority on toleration and individual freedom, it is not possible to remove values we don't like. Achieving collective action in a permanently contentious setting is a fundamentally different challenge than in other settings. Politics is the unavoidable consequence of conflicts in norms and values, the method we use to cooperate in the absence of agreed-upon criteria for the distribution of scarce resources. If citizens and leaders shared a common understanding on fundamental values, if differences of interpretation were rare, or if resources were abundant, the need for politics would disappear, for politics in the best sense is deliberating, bargaining and compromising among those who disagree.

Enter trust. The conditions that give rise to democratic politics are precisely those that reduce the likelihood of trust.[2] Francis Fukuyama, for example, provides this formulation: 'The ability to associate depends ... on the degree to which communities share norms and values and are able to subordinate individual interests to those of larger groups. Out of such shared values comes trust ....'[3] That is not the only way to describe trust. Fukuyama's is just one version amidst a literature that has grown considerably in the last decade as scholars, sociologists, philosophers, and social critics attempted to shed light on the widely observed phenomenon of declining trust in society. But it is reasonable to assume, and there is empirical evidence to support the claim, that trust develops more readily among like-minded individuals who share allegiances and common bonds. The relationship between trust and democratic politics is therefore problematic, marked by an inherent tension, characterized by inversely related circumstances. Trust thrives where politics does not. Like the arms suspended on a mobile, one moves in opposition to the other.

But that offers little reassurance to those who worry about the decline in trust now well documented throughout American society. One recent study reported, 'America is fast becoming a nation of strangers and this mistrust of each other is a major reason Americans have lost faith in the federal government and virtually every other major national institution.'[4] Reactions have followed a predictable formula: an analyst's alarmed response followed by the analyst's preferred solution. Trust can be restored by – take your pick – term limits on elected officials, balanced budgets, regulatory reform, reinventing government, campaign finance reform, responsible journalism, stronger political parties, more responsible elites, restrictions on lobbyists, vigorous local government, less government or more government.

This chapter explores the fundamental question of why trust matters in contemporary democracies. What benefits does trust provide? In a theory of government based heavily on an expectation that leaders will occasionally and even frequently misuse discretionary power, why should a decline in trust be worrisome?

J. Roland Pennock, the noted political theorist, describes modern leadership as consisting of four tasks or functions:

- Aiding the thoughts of others by identifying and pointing out problems for which political action is appropriate;
- Enabling opinions to be effective once they are formed; providing goals and sets of ideals which people can support;
- Obtaining the agreement of an effective coalition on any policy and establishing priorities;
- Translating the area of agreement into action.[5]

Leadership is the combination of all those tasks but the complexity of modern society and the growing scope of governmental action mean they are not all assigned to a single individual or office. They separate into various institutions and the relationships among those institutions and the individuals who inhabit them become, to some degree, formally constrained by their defined constitutional roles. Leadership thus becomes less personal and more institutional, a development with significant implications for analyzing the dynamics of the rise and fall of trust. The kind of trust that matters in this formal, specialized, and constitutionally constrained relationship is not the same as the one that emerges in a personal relationship. This political trust is fundamentally different both in its origins and purposes from that which develops among family, friends, and neighbors. There are many reasons why, as this chapter hopes to show, but one reason certainly is the difficulty of removing those values we don't like in our political relationships while relying upon compatible values in constructing our personal relationships.

There is another important implication. In the modern administrative state, the story of trust is the decision when and under what conditions we grant discretion to others. With only slight exaggeration, we might even claim that *the* dilemma of modern administrative leadership as it confronts the demands of democracy is establishing equilibrium between accountability and discretion, between setting limits on leaders' activities while allowing them the flexibility to act. If so, understanding trust in leaders goes to the heart of the everyday formation and implementation of public policy.[6]

Suspicion and Trust

And so contemporary discussion of declining trust in American political life is complicated at the outset. On the one hand, mistrust of political authorities, not trust, rests firmly within the political tradition of liberalism. The rationale for the origins of the state and the need for political leaders stem from a belief in a flawed human nature – a social nature to be sure, but also one that is hard-wired to calculate self-interest before the good of the whole. On the other hand, to say that mistrust has a place in the foundation of our political life is not to say that trust has no place. Although we would not want to pay the price of eliminating the conditions that require us to resort to politics, we do aspire to live in communities of trust where citizens support each other and leaders pursue a common good. The concern with declining trust is not misplaced. It is indeed worrisome when the recent trend in the polls shows a precipitous and steady decline in the percentages of those who 'trust government to do the right thing most of the time.' But it is more complicated than it first appears. In Janus-like fashion, we look both ways, adhering to political theories that feature mistrust of leaders as a basic tenet while lamenting the loss of trust. It is the paradox of American democracy.

It is also the paradox of American political leadership. Thomas Jefferson personified it. He may have actually created it, according to Joseph Ellis, one of his most perceptive biographers, who tried to take the measure of a man genuinely allergic to politics even as he continually immersed himself in it. In a culture that views political authority as a necessary evil, reluctance to assume leadership became a credential for leadership. Leaders must 'cloak the exercise of power from public view,' and make it 'appear to be a tamer and more innocuous power than it really is.' Ellis continues:

> If there is also an inherent disjunction between the ideals on which the nation is founded (i.e., individual freedom, equality of opportunity and popular sovereignty) and the imperatives of effective government, imperatives which require the capacity to coerce and discipline the undecided and faint of heart, then effective leadership, especially at the executive level must be capable of benign deception.

Jefferson fretted over power, mistrusted it, and provided the rationale to severely circumscribe it. The consequence, which Jefferson could not himself avoid, was the need to present arguments and marshal forces in a 'manipulative milieu.' The limits on power confronting the need to exercise power; a perspective that views authority warily while criticizing those who lack the skills to accomplish their ends in such a constrained environment; the practice of benign deception co-existing with the need to communicate truthfully – all result in a leadership 'style based on the capacity to rest comfortably with contradictions.'[7]

Trust lies at the heart of this paradox. To understand its place in a theory of political leadership, we must tolerate a fair amount of ambiguity and contradiction. It is possible, for example, to discern two quite different explanations for the loss of trust in leaders. One is that public officials pursue their self-interest to the detriment of others or in opposition to a general public interest. In politics or in their personal lives, people do not typically trust those who do not share their interests or acknowledge them. They may cooperate, but the basis of the cooperation is not trust. Loss of trust in this sense is mistrust, a judgment that the motives of others are not transparent or are in outright opposition to one's own interest.

The other explanation for the loss of trust is that public officials are not effective. Though leaders may share our interests and work to realize them, they too often fail. Citizens do not place their faith in them nor do they believe they have the ability to do what they promise even with the best of intentions. Loss of trust in this sense is a loss of confidence. This lack of faith may broaden to become a lack of confidence in 'the system,' the political and economic institutions in which public officials, however well intentioned and capable, find themselves. Writing in 1980, in the wake of the Vietnam War, the Watergate scandals, and President Carter's apparent inability to resolve the Iranian hostage crisis, the twin afflictions of inflation and unemployment, and the energy shortage, James L. Sundquist described a 'crisis of competence.' It let him to conclude, 'The performance of the government has fallen far short of what the people have expected and have a right to expect.'[8] More recently, Joseph S. Nye, Jr. and several colleagues asked why people don't trust government and answered in terms of declining confidence among citizens in the ability of leaders to cope with the demands of the democratic process.[9] In short, declining trust results from a judgment that leaders competently pursue their own interests, or incompetently pursue the public interest, or are essentially hamstrung by poorly designed institutions. All these perspectives are found within our political theories and in the diagnosis of contemporary ills, often so entangled with each other that analysis is impossible.

But if trust is part and parcel of the paradox, it also is part of the solution. The inherent problem of democracy in the administrative state is reconciling the political imperative of accountability with the managerial imperatives of flexibility and responsiveness. Our political theories advise us to restrain authority. Liberal thought begins with suspicion of power and it is only a slight exaggeration to say that the modern history of Western government is one of defining its limits. In America, the effort found its clearest expression in the Constitution – a set of formal checks and balances that ingrained in our political culture a dependence on procedures and organizational forms as the primary means to limit the actions of those in government. 'The constant aim,' Madison wrote, 'is to divide and arrange the several offices in such a manner that they may be a check on the other – that the private interest of every individual may be a sentinel over the public rights.'[10]

Our organizational theories tell us something quite different. Leaders must have discretion. Those who write the laws and administer them cannot possibly foresee the many complications that might arise. Society has become too complex and the scope of government too wide and varied. Organizational structures must be organic and dynamic rather than rigid and mechanistic. Consequently, the ways in which we seek the perfectly legitimate goal of political accountability are often at cross-purposes with effective leadership. Elaborate structures and procedures may protect the public against abuses of authority, but they may also result in the pathologies of inefficiency and risk aversion associated with excessive bureaucracy.

Trust helps resolve the predicament. As it varies, so does the tension between the competing imperatives. A high level of trust does not eliminate the need for accountability but it can make the methods for achieving it less intrusive, providing discretion for leaders and a greater willingness to delegate. Chester Barnard, a management theorist, long ago referred to a zone of indifference, an area in which individuals would accept the direction of someone in authority.[11] Similarly, we might imagine a zone of discretion, the size of which depends upon the level of trust among the citizens, their elected representatives, and administrators. One of the most basic problems in leadership, at least within the prevailing theory of modern government, cannot be understood without a better appreciation of how trust expands the zone and mistrust causes it to contract. In the words of literary critic Gabriel Josipovici writing in a much different context, the problem 'is how to keep suspicion from turning into cynicism and trust from turning into facileness. Trust without suspicion is the recipe for a false and meritricious art; but suspicion without trust is the recipe for a shallow and empty art.'[12] Substitute 'politics' for art and Josipovici has deftly posed the challenge for understanding modern political leadership: a balance of suspicion and trust.

The Modern View and Its Origins

Locke's Prerogative

If Machiavelli alerted us to the need for power and the virtue of exercising it, Locke alerted us to its vices and the need to constrain it. The seventeenth century English philosopher profoundly shaped modern views of politics, the individual and the state. The broad range of his writings on so many subjects has been extensively analyzed and his influence on the American founding, its emphasis on rights, freedom, and equality meticulously set forth.[13] It is, therefore, a matter of convenience only that permits an intensive and selective examination of a few particular passages. But those passages – especially Chapter XIV in *The Second Treatise of Government* – are remarkable for the way they anticipate the dilemma of leadership in today's modern state. They are gateways. Through them we enter into an enlightening analysis of discretion and the duties and obligations of those placed in positions of 'public trust.'

Notwithstanding Locke's deserved reputation for constructing theories limiting governmental power he conceded that inevitably officials would have to
make decisions in the absence of clear directives.

> Many things there are which the law can no means provide for; and those must
> necessarily be left to the discretion of him that has the executive power in his
> hands, to be ordered by him as the public good and advantage shall require ...
> [T]here is a latitude left to the executive power to do many things of choice
> which the laws do not prescribe.

Locke called this 'prerogative,' and he defined it as 'nothing but the power of
doing good without a rule.' He went even further. Officials might at times
legitimately contravene the law, acting with discretion not only when the law
is silent but also when the law stands in the way of the community's benefit.
Under some circumstances, a 'strict and rigid observation of the laws may do
harm,' and the obligation to serve the public good could require the official to
violate the letter of the law in the name of a greater good.[14]

But this was no license, for prerogative must be exercised only in pursuit
of the public good (as opposed to the official's own personal benefit) and only
when the people trust the official. Locke thus constructs a critical linkage
between trust and the common good, providing a key proposition joining together the ability of the leader to garner trust with the obligation to use that
trust in a particular way. The 'end of government is the good of the community.' As long as the people judge that to be the goal of the official, they will
trust him. Trust becomes both cause and effect. It enables the use of prerogative; the legitimate use of prerogative engenders trust. Drawing from the history of his native England, Locke found:

> ... prerogative was always largest in the hands of our wisest and best princes,
> because the people, observing the whole tendency of their actions to be the
> public good ... (and) it was visible that the main of their conduct tended to
> nothing but the care of the public. The people, therefore, finding reason to be
> satisfied with these princes whenever they acted without or contrary to the letter
> of the law, acquiesced in what they did, and without the least complaint let them
> enlarge their prerogative as they pleased, judging rightly that they did nothing
> herein to the prejudice of their laws since they acted comfortably to the founda-
> tion and end of all laws – the public good.[15]

Locke's justification of prerogative rests on two pillars. First, to be sure,
the exact determination of the public good is not a simple matter and naturally
there are differences of opinion among the people themselves as well as between the people and the officials. That is the essence of political debate. But
short of discovering a clear public interest, we may still impose upon leaders
the obligation not to act only in their own self-interest. The middle ground, if

that is not too misleading a term, is impartiality – that is, a detachment or disinterestedness, an assurance that at a minimum the official will not use his office or the power of prerogative to advance one interest over another. This is an integral aspect of Locke's philosophy, originating with the fundamental argument over why people would ever leave behind the primitive liberty they possess in the 'state of nature' to form a political society and live under its regulations and restrictions. They would do so, he argues, because even though the law of nature is understandable to all rational creatures, 'men, being biased by their own interest as well as ignorant for want of studying it, are not apt to allow of it as a law binding to them in the application of it to their particular cases.' Moreover, 'in the state of nature there wants a known and indifferent judge with authority to determine all differences according to established law.'[16] The virtue of impartiality is a prerequisite for trust and the exercise of prerogative.

Second, it is essential to understand how Locke distinguished legitimate political power from other forms of power. The concept of prerogative is a distinctly political phenomenon. It pertains to the particular responsibilities of political leaders. In describing it, Locke thus provides insight into his more general point about the separation of the public and private realms of society – and hence the inference we can draw about the distinction between political and personal trust.

Locke first distinguishes political power from parental. Parents use power in accordance with the law of nature for the 'help, instruction, and preservation of their offspring.'[17] It extends over those whose capacity for reason is not yet fully developed. But the power does not extend 'itself to the ends and jurisdictions of that which is political.' For that we have the distinctly different political power voluntarily granted by those who possess reason to those who will govern them 'with the express or tacit trust that it shall be employed for their good and preservation of their property.'[18] Finally, there is despotic power, a clearly illegitimate power because it does not serve the good of the people and hence they could not have reasonably consented to it (since no rational being would consent to being harmed). Contrasting the three versions brings the contours of the political realm into sharp relief: 'he that shall consider the distinct rise and extent, and the different ends of these several powers, will plainly see that paternal power comes as far short of that of the magistrate as despotical power exceeds it.'[19] Prerogative is an exercise of power that makes sense only in political society. In despotic societies, the public good, upon which prerogative depends for its legitimacy, is not a motivating factor.

Trust was indeed at the heart of Locke's liberalism. In a polity of individual freedom and constrained government, it was impossible for him to imagine interactions without granting at least some leeway to those with whom we interact, either citizen to citizen or citizen to ruler. To state the case even more emphatically, we must trust others if we aspire to anything more than the most primitive state of relations. John Dunn's analysis of Locke's trust led him to conclude, 'Credally, just as much as politically, therefore, men's existence requires them to put their trust in what may well in practice prove to betray them.'[20] In Locke's world, according to Dunn, life is full of hazard, which is another way of saying it is full of possibility. Without risk, the potential of human life is limited; without trust, it is difficult if not impossible to accept some level of risk.

Locke's legacy also helps us understand that as we move from the family and civil society to the distinctly different realm of political society, the basis for trust shifts. 'It depends,' Dunn argues, 'on many different sorts of considerations: on the contingencies of individual disposition, of the prevailing culture of a particular community and of the practical structures of material interests which are at issue.'[21] It depends, in other words, on a mix of rational and affective factors, on calculations of mutual interest as well as the suspension of calculation and strategizing with those we have come to trust. Locke's depiction of trust is a richly textured one, often in stark contrast to the contemporary analyses.

But it did leave at least one glaring void. When leaders violate the trust placed in them – when they show themselves to be untrustworthy by not pursuing the public good – there must be a readily available recourse other than appeals to heaven. Dunn once again usefully presents the predicament:

> Human beings must and do trust their rulers. They trust them on the whole far beyond the latter's' deserts, and to the damage of their own interest. But in the last instance they retain (and indeed have no power to abandon) the right and duty to judge for themselves how far their trust has been deserved and where and when it has been betrayed. And if they judge it to be betrayed, they have every right to act in concert and seek to re-establish for themselves a form of sovereign power in which they can, once again, rationally place their trust.[22]

The task of finding a method of removal takes us to a different stage in the development of political trust, one that requires consideration of processes and institutional design. It takes us to a different time and place.

Jay's Pirouette

The problem finds classic expression in *The Federalist Papers*, specifically number 64, an essay that draws far less attention than many of the others in that classic work. In describing the treaty-making provisions of the Constitution, John Jay, diplomat and future secretary of state, stumbles into a perfect illustration of our rather complicated perspective on trust in political life. His immediate purpose is to justify the apparently large amount of discretion given to the executive to negotiate treaties while arguing at the same time that the power is circumscribed. It's a variation of the delicate dance found throughout *The Federalist Papers* – and characteristic of much of our political theory.

The negotiation of treaties, an important function of today's national government, was understandably an even greater concern for the citizens of the new republic. Here was a classic leadership problem in a constrained constitutional order. Committing the new nation to the defense of another sovereign entity was a decision with high stakes, even as it promised some additional security for the United States by committing others to assist in our defense. Governmental actions of such magnitude surely fell into the category of those that required checks and balances. But even lesser treaties over trading privileges or boundaries or the exchange of land seemed to vest an uncomfortable degree of power in the hands of those sitting around the table, not the people at large. Jay, the seasoned and practical diplomat, knew, however, that the people could not sit around the table. Negotiators must negotiate, hammer out the details, master the fine points, compromise and bargain over the precise language. Moreover, adversaries on the other side of the table needed to know that the promises made by the representatives from the new republic would be honored. Diplomats, although surely answerable to the people, had to be more than mere ciphers and functionaries. How then to grant the leaders power while living up to the Constitution's scheme of limiting power?

Jay's first strategy was to explain why citizens should have faith in their leaders to negotiate a favorable treaty. The Constitution, he argued, ensures the selection of the 'most enlightened and respectable' public officials who, 'having no private interests distinct from that of the nation ... will be under no temptations to neglect the latter.' And '[i]f the observation be well founded that wise kings will always be served by wise administrators ... so will their appointments bear at least equal marks of discretion and discernment.'[23] Throughout government ranks will be people whose integrity and virtue will allow us to entrust them with the discretion necessitated, in the case of treaty making, by the demands for 'secrecy and dispatch.' Wise and virtuous, they could be trusted. But if that is insufficient reassurance, Jay goes on to point out, consider that their interests will be no different from the citizenry. They will live under the same treaty as everyone else. How could reasonable, skilled, and wise officials negotiate a treaty not in their interest – and therefore not in the people's interest?

But in the essay's conclusion, Jay's dance culminates abruptly in an incredible pirouette.

> In short, as the Constitution has taken the utmost care that they shall be men of
> talents, and integrity, we have reason to be persuaded that the treaties they make
> will be as advantageous as, all circumstances considered, could be made; and so
> far as the fear of punishment and disgrace can operate, that motive to good
> behaviour is amply afforded by the article on the subject of impeachments.[24]

We trust our wise and prudent leaders, but only so far. What the Constitution gives in the name of trust and administrative necessity, it stands ready to withdraw in the name of distrust and political accountability. The artistry and grace of Jay's pirouette is elegant. Some discretion is necessary; it is a managerial imperative. The negotiation of effective treaties requires secrecy and dispatch. To one degree or another so do many of the functions of modern government, such as the setting of regulations, the enforcement of laws, and the day-to-day contacts with clients. However, we grant that authority – that prerogative – only if two conditions apply, both of them alluded to by Jay.

The first is the requirement that boundaries to the prerogative remain firmly in place. Political trust is always conditional. Citizens should never unconditionally trust leaders in the same way they unconditionally trust family, friends, and even neighbors. The prospect of doing so is unnerving, calling to mind images of autocracy, despotism, or regimes in which leaders have acquired and inevitably abused unconditional trust. Moreover, a measure of distrust is prudent as Algernon Sydney explained in 1698 because:

> Men are so subject to vices and passions that they stand in need of some re-
> straints in every condition; but especially when they are in power. The rage of a
> private man may be pernicious to one or few of his neighbors; but the fury of an
> unlimited prince would drive whole nations into ruin. And those very men, who
> have lived modestly when they had little power, have often proved the most
> savage when they thought nothing able to resist their rage.[25]

In the absence of boundaries around the discretion we grant to leaders – in the absence of insurance policies such as in Jay's discussion in the article on impeachments – we are less inclined to grant discretion or to grant trust in a political sense.

The second factor that determines the boundaries of discretion is the nature of the leaders themselves, their wisdom, and integrity, as well as the compatibility of their interests and those of the citizens. Jay's defense of the institutional design of the Constitution, particularly his reference to the article on impeachment, depended on demonstrating that an insurance policy against the violation of trust did in fact exist. But he emphasized much more how the design of the Constitution fostered (without guaranteeing) the recruitment to public office of 'enlightened and respectable' leaders who surely possess at least a modicum of benign intent. The apparent purpose of Jay's task was to inspire trust in leaders themselves, but in linking the development of trust to the proper design of institutions, Jay was also implying that political trust was in good part a trust in the institutions as well.

Jay's essay encapsulates the modern view of trust and leadership, blending the personal and the institutional. On the one hand, citizens need to trust their leaders and they do so when they determine that leaders share their interests, as well as their values, and are wise and capable enough to achieve what they set out to do. On the other hand, the trust is bounded and conditional, the risk moderated by a kind of institutional insurance policy that acts as an additional 'motive to good behavior.'

Ward Just, the contemporary political novelist, captures the dynamic in a particularly vivid and metaphorical scene at a masquerade ball of the Washington, DC power elite, as one of the women wonders about one of the men.

> Virginia Spears was avid for a peek behind the mask, thinking that she was staring into a man's soul when she was only looking at a second mask, the one that was even more untrustworthy than the first. She was interested in both dance and dancer, and it would be important to keep her focused on the first, where the feet go when you're preparing a pirouette, not the spin itself, not the actual doing of it, but the preparation for it, the process.[26]

And Jay's pirouette draws us to the dance and the dancer, the movement and the person, the form and the substance. Regrettably, though, contemporary discussions of trust seem to have lost the intricacies of the legacy handed down by Locke and Jay. What they joined together, others have lately torn asunder.

The Limitations of the Modern View

The topic of trust is not immune to the trend that pervades the social science and social philosophy today. In its broadest terms, it is, in Peter Berkowitz's words, 'the restless ambition to bring the entirety of moral and political life, in all its complexity and its many-sidedness, under the sway of a single cause or an exclusive principle.'[27] That of course is not a tendency unique to this day and age. But its current manifestation is the attempt to explain most human behavior in terms of the single-minded pursuit of self-interest. Humans are rational decision-makers; the now familiar argument goes. Life is a series of choices, in both the public and private realms, and the calculus driving the choices is a weighing of the costs and the benefits of each alternative. The outcome is the selection of the alternative with the highest pay-off or the maximum utility. Beginning with this assumption about micro or individual behavior, social scientists go on to create elaborate models of collective action by aggregating the multitudes of individual rational choices.

Trust, however, poses something of a problem for this mono-causal approach to social behavior.

On the one hand, trust as a feature of human behavior can be squeezed into the models of rational choice without too much difficulty. Simply, people trust others when they determine that the pay-off is worth the risk of trusting another person. We grant discretion to someone, calculating that the person will deliver benefits that made the risk worthwhile. 'Trust is rational,' according to William Bianco.[28] The late James Coleman, the sociologist, defines trust as 'nothing more or less than the considerations a rational actor applies when deciding to place a bet.'[29] When the focus shifts to the implications for collective action, trust becomes important as a way of facilitating cooperation. The problems that typically frustrate collective action, such as the tendency to 'free-ride' on the sacrifices of other citizens, are easier to overcome in societies where levels of trust are high. Individuals more willingly grant leeway to others without having to depend upon coercive government, or highly codified and carefully negotiated legal contracts. To use the terminology of the rational choice model, the 'transaction costs' are lower. In settings with high levels of trust, cooperation with mutually beneficial consequences (a positive sum game) occurs more often than conflict (a zero-sum game).

On the other hand, such characterizations of trust sanitize the concept, reducing it to something much less than it deserves. Francis Fukuyama is one critic who rejects the rational choice depiction of trust.[30] Culture matters, he says, because it transmits the values of the society developed over time and passed on from generation to generation. The character of the community, its norms, traditions and cohesiveness foster trust. Trust is anything but another form of the pursuit of self-interest. On the contrary, we trust those who seem to acknowledge the legitimacy of our interests and give evidence that they hold a set of obligations requiring self-sacrifice. Trust may actually be the suspension of self-interest, better understood as a derivative of the community's values and norms.[31] Oliver Williamson, an economist who fully understands and appreciates the power of the rational choice model, is himself cautious about using it to analyze trust. He advises removing the term trust from models of behavior based on economic gain and reserving the term for those 'special personal relations that would be seriously degraded if a calculative orientation were "permitted."'[32] March and Olsen issue a similar warning.

> The core idea of trust is that it is not based on an expectation of its justification. When trust is justified by expectations of positive reciprocal consequences, it is simply another version of economic exchange ... [Trust instead] is sustained by socialization into the structure of rules, and rarely considered as a deliberate willful action. Thus, trust can be undermined by persistent untrustworthiness, but it is more likely to be undermined by coming to see the granting of trust as

part of a voluntary contractual agreement, rather than as one of the normal obligations of political life.[33]

Both perspectives have difficulties, however. To conceive of trust as merely the product of rational calculation is to strip it of any significance as one of the 'normal obligations of political life.' If it is merely another version of economic exchange, there seems little reason to complicate matters by calling it trust. Simple economic analysis of cost–benefit, utility maximization is the more parsimonious explanation. By the same token, to conceive of trust in the political realm only as a product of affective (rather than rational) relationships and contingent upon consensus on fundamental values and norms renders it problematic for modern pluralistic societies. Trust would be an unattainable ideal.

We seem caught in a vise, squeezed on one side by theories with cramped explanations of human behavior and impoverished views of politics and on the other by imaginary, unreal societies with perfect harmony of norms. Is there a way of 'avoiding the Scylla of rational choice perspectives on trust (which are often but extended studies on the condition of confidence in any interaction) and the Charybdis of a normative perspective (which would apotheosize trust as the conscience of a collective society ...'?[34]

The rough outlines of such a perspective begin with premises handed down to us by Locke and Jay. A political version of trust is not the same as the personal, for we trust political leaders and other individuals in their capacity as citizens on a different basis than we do family, friends, and neighbors. There are many reasons why, but surely the most fundamental is that our political relationships are purposive, limited, and functional. They exist within institutions, formally designed and constitutionally proscribed – and consequently detached in significant ways from the individual who occupies the office. The commitment to these institutions develops over time and ultimately constitutes the political capital of society. Certain kinds of institutional arrangements, by the way they structure relationships among individuals, make trust more or less likely to occur. When they succeed, citizens gain confidence in them and learn to trust the institutions, their structures, and their processes. Citizens keep their eye on the dance as well as the dancer.

The point is a complex but significant one. The consensus among individuals – the basis for political capital in society – is a commitment to the design of the institution and the processes it provides for the fair and just resolution of conflict. It suggests a counter-intuitive proposition. Political trust may actually depend on more rather than less structural and procedural complexity. By virtue of their particular design, certain institutions make us more willing to trust others in a political setting by protecting us from the harm that can result from a violated trust. Our intuitive understanding by contrast is that institutional complexity, elaborately codified rules, or complicated procedures are indications of weak norms and low levels of trust. But, that conventional view may be accurate only to the degree that we view trust in interpersonal terms or only to the degree that we accept Fukuyama's formulation of strong cultures as the necessary condition for trust. In the political as opposed to the personal, institutional complexity may promote trust.[35]

But it is also a modest, limited version of trust. Political trust is not the same as the unconditional trust we place in our friends and family. And the virtue it depends upon, while a demanding one that should not be underestimated, is nevertheless tailored for the political realm, to the forums where we cooperate on fair terms, committed to reasoned presentations of opposing ideas, trusting that others, whether fellow citizens or officials, will do their part as well, even as disagreement persists as a permanent condition of democratic society.

The implications for leadership theory are significant. The foundation of political trust in modern democracies depends not only on what social scientists refer to as behavioral factors, such as rational calculations of whether a given trust is worth the risk and affective judgments about the benign intent of the person to be trusted. It depends also on structural factors, such as the competence of officials to work within the institutional constraints of their particular positions while fulfilling a broad set of standards consistent with basic democratic principles. To maneuver effectively within the dilemma of leadership in a democracy, political leaders must be shrewd managers as well as faithful democrats, skillful as well as principled.

By way of illustration, consider two cases: the delegation of authority from Congress to administrative agencies in the area of environmental policy; and the Keating Five scandal when Senators interceded in an investigation of a savings and loan executive who had contributed to their election campaigns. The cases bring us into the everyday life of politics and public policy, revealing the sources of trust and the responsibilities of officials if they wish to preserve it.

Legislative Delegation and Administrative Discretion: The Case of Environmental Standards Under the Clean Air Act

Delegation of decision-making authority from Congress to administrators raises a difficult question for leadership in the administrative state. What are the bounds of legitimate action by leaders vested with discretion? The issue also helps clarify how the level of trust in institutions and their leaders influences the willingness of citizens to tolerate a degree of discretion. When trust increases, discretion becomes less problematic; when mistrust increases, emphasis shifts to accountability and narrowing the range of discretion.

The controversy has re-emerged on a number of fronts, especially in the regulatory arena, where some observers attribute the decline in trust to a lack of confidence in political institutions. Supreme Court Justice Stephen Breyer for one has argued:

> Respect for decisions as authoritative is not easy to create in this era of political distrust ... Still, it seems to me that public respect depends not only upon the perception of public participation but also, in part, upon an organization's successful accomplishment of a mission that satisfies an important need ... [T]he authority or legitimacy of a particular regulatory action depends in part upon its technical sophistication, and in part upon its conformity with the law, and both parts help to determine the extent of public confidence in the regulator.[36]

In *Breaking the Vicious Circle*, a book published before his appointment to the Supreme Court, Breyer sees the solution not in limiting the discretionary authority per se but in expanding the capacity of decision-makers to make rational, technically sound calculations about health risks and the costs of reducing them.

But there is another response to the concern over administrative discretion. It lies in the growing receptivity to claims that Congress has unconstitutionally ceded too much of its law-making power to others. The 'nondelegation doctrine' has been around for quite some time, as we shall see, but its force has been tempered over the years by 'a practical understanding that in our increasingly complex society, replete with ever changing and more technical problems, Congress simply cannot do its job absent an ability to delegate power under broad general objectives.'[37] One symptom of mistrust in contemporary politics is the apparent willingness of the justices to take a harder look at the scope of authority exercised by administrative agencies – to narrow their range of discretion and force Congress to 'do its job' rather than pawning it off on others. For one legal scholar, this is indeed a fundamental question of democratic theory and accountability. The problem is Congress's:

> propensity not to make politically controversial decisions – to leave them instead to others, most often others who are not elected or effectively controlled by those who are. If we can just get our legislators to legislate we'll be able to understand their goals well enough. I'm not saying we may not still end up with a fair number of clowns as representatives, but at least then it will be because clowns are what we deserve.[38]

Though a sometimes legalistic and arcane topic not typically discussed in the context of leadership, the tension between the political imperative of accountability and the managerial imperative of discretion, between democracy

and bureaucracy, is at the heart of many leadership questions in modern democratic states. Despite deep roots in political theory and decades of debate on
specific policy questions, the currently confused state of affairs is best captured by Dennis Thompson's assessment. 'Neither democratic theory nor democratic practice has yet discovered a form of administrative responsibility that
would let democrats comfortably consort with bureaucrats in the governing of
society.'[39] The long-running debate over the scope of administrative authority, made all the more acute by present-day realities of governance, is one of
the most obvious manifestations.

Not surprisingly, John Locke – whose declarations support so many of our
democratic practices – set the stage. For him it was an easy call. He was un-
equivocal. 'The Legislative cannot transfer the Power of Making Laws to any
other hands.' Elected representatives dilute their authority (and by extension
the people's authority) by transferring their responsibilities to others. Accountability requires clear lines of responsibility. The people have consented to be
ruled by those they have chosen. The legislature is thus their agent and the
agent may not modify its role by creating another agent and establishing itself
as the principal. If the legislature does assign others the power to make laws,
the people need not obey them since they had not given their consent. 'These
are the Bounds of trust that is put in them by Society, and the Law of God and
Nature, have set to the legislative Power of every Commonwealth, in all Forms
of Government.'[40]

Locke's admonition had a clear logic, and later during the founding of the
American republic, the authors of *The Federalist Papers* embraced the separation of powers with enthusiasm. Establishing different branches to perform
the distinct functions of legislating, adjudicating, and administering – an approach traced to the influence of Montesquieu as well as Locke – was an
ingenious institutional design not only for accomplishing the ends of government but also limiting its power.[41] The plan depended upon each branch jeal-
ously guarding its assigned role. The legislature would vigorously protect its
own powers against encroachment from other branches. By defending its own
turf, it would check the aggrandizing tendencies of the other branches.

But the reality of governing presented inconvenient complications; and
practicality, never far from the thoughts of the Founders, led at least some of
them to conclude that shading of the bright lines of separation would occasionally be prudent. For John Jay, those previously mentioned details of treaty-
making once again provided a good example. The opponents of the Constitution were displeased with the treaty-making provision, 'because, as the treaties, when made, are to have the force of laws, they should be made only by
men invested with legislative authority.' The executive did not have nor should
have legislative or law-making power. But Jay foresaw the complications that

would result from a rigid interpretation of the Lockean principle and met the critics head on:

> These gentlemen seem not to consider that the judgments of our courts, and the commissions constitutionally given by our governor, are as valid and as binding on all persons whom they concern as the laws passed by our legislature. All constitutional acts of power, whether in the executive or the judicial department, have as much legal validity and obligation as if they proceeded from the legislature …. It surely does not follow that because they have given the power of making laws to the legislature, that therefore they should likewise give them power to do every act of sovereignty by which the citizens are to be bound and affected.[42]

The dilemma is still with us today. On the morning of November 7, 2000, Solicitor General Seth Waxmann and attorney Edward Warren met in the august setting of the U.S. Supreme Court to argue the case of *Browner* v. *American Trucking, et al*. In this rarefied legal atmosphere, they did not invoke Locke and Jay, but they surely could have, for the issue of legislative delegation of power was front and center – although in a very specific manner unimaginable to either of the long-gone writers.[43] Acting in his customary role of representing the government's position, Waxmann defended the Environmental Protection Agency and its Director, Carol Browner, who had recently decided upon a standard for ozone in the air. Citing a raft of scientific evidence and advice from the Clean Air Scientific Advisory Committee (CASAC), Browner had set the standard at 0.08 parts per million. Her prerogative – indeed, according to Waxmann, her obligation and duty – derived from the Clean Air Act of 1970 (and subsequent amendments in 1977 and 1990) that charged her with regulating pollution to 'a level requisite necessary to protect public health.'

Warren represented the American Trucking Association and several other petitioners. On their behalf, he rejected the EPA's claim and argued that the Act was an unconstitutional delegation of power from Congress. It vested too much discretionary power in an unelected official. 'Protecting public health' was far too vague and broad to serve as a guiding criterion from the legislative body. Congress had effectively but improperly given Browner the power to write her own law, and Warren wanted to discern the basis upon which she had set the standard. Since ozone was a 'non-threshold pollutant,' meaning that some risk to health exists at any level of exposure, and since her charge was to protect the public health, wouldn't 0.07ppm, or 0.06ppm, or even zero be a more effective standard in ensuring public health? On the other hand, if some factors, such as cost or feasibility, prevented the director from imposing a stricter standard, wouldn't a more relaxed standard such as 0.10ppm, or 0.11ppm or even 0.15ppm be just as easily justified? What precisely was the reason for the 0.08ppm level? Did it derive from legislative guidance? Was the determining factor at least 'intelligible' (a basis used in previous court . decisions when the legislation appeared to give only general guidance)? For all intents and purposes, the EPA Director could choose whatever standard she wished, according to Warren, and that was too much discretion and too little accountability.[44]

The Appeals Court for the District of Columbia had agreed. Two of the three judges concluded, 'EPA's formulation of its policy judgment leaves it free to pick any point between zero and a hair below the concentrations yielding London's Killer Fog.'[45] And now the nine justices on the Supreme Court would decide whether Browner's zone of discretion was too wide.

The Clean Air Act stands as surely one of the most far-reaching pieces of legislation ever. Compliance costs reached half a trillion dollars per year. Benefits included the annual prevention of 45,00 deaths, 13,000 heart attacks, and 7,000 strokes.[46] If the Supreme Court agreed with the Appeals Court and found the Act or one of its provisions unconstitutional, the ruling would have enormous significance for environmental policy. But the stakes were even higher. The Clean Air Act was typical of the so-called 'new regulation.' In the 1960s and 1970s, regulatory policy expanded from basic oversight of economic and financial markets to managing social and health risks. The purpose and scope of regulation broadened considerably, embracing such matters as worker safety, medical treatment, consumer protection, and transportation. 'Not only does the new regulation directly touch more lives than does the old,' Shep Melnick concluded, 'but officials are less likely to see their job as promoting the effective management of one sector of the economy.'[47] One result was hostility between the business community and the regulators. Another was 'lengthy statutes … with specific standards, deadlines, and procedures.' Though courts had previously found fault with various EPA decisions, they had done so without reaching the far more serious conclusion that the Act itself was unconstitutional. Should the Court rule against EPA on those grounds in this case, it would potentially be open season on many other regulatory standards under this new regime.

It would also be a departure from nearly all the Court's precedents. The Court had never actually rejected the nondelegation doctrine, but justices rarely invoked it. In fact, in only two cases did it provide the basis for the controlling opinions, both of them coming in 1935 as the Court reined in some of the New Deal legislation, first in *Panama Refining Company* v. *Ryan* and then in *Schecter Poultry Corporation* v. *United States*.[48, 49] The effect of those rulings on the course of jurisprudence was in many respects minimal, serving only to reassure everyone that in the eyes of the Court, Congress may not give its power to others but apparently establishing a very high threshold for ruling against legislation on those grounds. The 1935 rulings were the exceptions.

More typical of the Court's approach was the case of *Chevron v. National Resources Defense Council* (1984), which also dealt with the EPA's authority under the Clean Air Act. 'When Congress's intent is clear,' the Justices ruled, 'that is the end of the matter, for the Court as well as the agency must give effect to the unambiguously expressed intent of Congress.' When Congress has been unclear, however, and that is more often going to be the case, 'the question for the Court is whether the agency's answer is based on a permissible construction of the statute.' Was the agency's finding 'reasonable' and 'intelligible'?[50] In the District of Columbia Appeals Court's decision on *American Trucking, et al. v. EPA*, the dissenting judge had taken precisely that approach, refusing to question the constitutionality of the Clean Air Act. His brethren in the majority, he believed, had ignored 'the last half century of Supreme Court nondelegation jurisprudence, apparently viewing these permissive precedents' – such as Chevron – 'as mere exceptions to the rule laid down 64 years ago' in Schecter.[51]

Recognition that delegation of authority is necessary does not mean that the separation of powers doctrine has been jettisoned, nor does it mean that Congress has abdicated its power and administrative agencies have a free license. Administrative discretion has occasionally, even frequently, been found to be improper. But the Court developed criteria other than the nondelegation principle for such findings. For example, administrative acts could not be 'arbitrary and capricious.' More comfortable with judging the fairness of administrative acts and the procedures used to arrive at decisions, the courts avoided substantive review for the most part.[52]

But political and judicial attitudes shift, and although the decline in trust cannot be the full explanation for taking the non-delegation doctrine off the shelf, it surely has played a role. The arguments from scholars who pressed the issue of nondelegation gradually crept into the public debate. Political scientist Theodore Lowi's highly influential 1969 book (revised in 1979), *The End of Liberalism*, was a broad attack on the transfer of legislative authority to administrative agencies. Some delegation is of course necessary, but it should be minimal because it is the equivalent of policy without law, 'pathological, and criticizable at the point where it comes to be considered a good thing in itself, flowing to administrators without guides, checks, safeguards.'[53] The consequence was an erosion of liberal principles of accountability, the institutionalization of special interests in administrative agencies 'captured' by those they are supposed to regulate in the name of a broader public interest. John Ely entitled his 1980 book *Democracy and Distrust* and called for renewed attention to the non-delegation doctrine, rejecting arguments that the legislature cannot decide technical and complex matters.[54] In an often cited 1982 law review article, three scholars pleaded with the courts to 'nullify all delegations of legislative authority ... If the agency could not trace its action to a specific delegation far more detailed than an exhortation to regulate in the public interest, then the court would overturn both the agency action and the original statute delegating the legislative authority.'[55] In the pages of *The Harvard Law Review* in 1994, Gary Lawson did not mince words. 'The modern administrative state openly flouts almost every important structural precept of the American constitutional order.'[56] David Schoenbrod writing specifically about environmental legislation echoed their pleas. 'The Supreme Court should declare unconstitutional all delegation of legislative power or, if the Court thinks that effective government requires some delegation, it should permit only delegation of uncontroversial details.'[57] Trust – or mistrust – was at the core of his analysis.

> Opposition to delegation also generally is assumed to reflect a belief that the legislative branch of government is more trustworthy than the executive. But my opposition to delegation stems from distrust of both legislative and executive officials. Precisely because of this distrust I want legislators and the president to make law only by taking publicly recorded positions, as they must when they enact or sign statutes, rather than by pressuring agencies in private, as they do after they delegate.[58]

On February 27, 2001, a unanimous Supreme Court issued a complex opinion upholding the constitutionality of the Clean Air Act. Writing for the Court, Justice Scalia – not a friend of the administrative state by any means – acknowledged the need for delegation and cited a number of the key precedents, such as *Chevron* and *Mistretta*, which gave latitude to Congress.[59] At the same time, however, the Court sent the standards for ozone back to the EPA on grounds that the agency had ignored one part of the statute that seemed to limit its discretion while resting its claim to authority solely on another part of the Act. By one interpretation, the Court adhered to the conventional reading of the nondelegation doctrine, which is to say it bypassed the opportunity to reinvigorate it. On the other hand, according to one scholar, 'The court that did not deliver a knock-out blow to administrative agencies on non-delegation grounds did show a "harder look" approach to judicial review of administrative action.'[60] Jurisprudence typically moves in these kinds of incremental steps, but the words of Justice Thomas in a concurring opinion signaled that the issue is not over. 'On a future day, however, I would be willing to address the question whether our delegation jurisprudence has strayed too far from our Founders' understanding of separation of powers.'[61]

The point here is not that statutory specificity is better or worse at ensuring effective leadership in democratic societies or that it somehow might destabilize the current balance between discretion and accountability. No matter what direction jurisprudence takes, responsible leadership at any level in the administrative state, now more than ever, requires clarity in explaining complicated decisions to the citizenry. The argument *for* the nondelegation doctrine is based on the principle that citizens forced to live under laws should understand the rationale behind the decisions and be able to hold someone accountable for them. The argument *against* a rigid application of the nondelegation doctrine depends upon the same principles but recognizes that administrative leaders unavoidably are also political leaders charged with managing complex organizations central to modern democracy. In their meticulous critique of the Environmental Protection Agency, Marc Landy and his co-authors advise:

> The success of a republic depends upon the capacities of institutions as well as those of its citizens ... [T]o gain the trust of its citizens, government must ensure that they understand and appreciate its efforts. Developing governmental capacity of this sort is the long run institutional counterpoint to civic education. For this to occur, civil servants need to be both technically and politically expert and perceived as such by citizens. Perpetuation of institutional memory, recruitment and retention of skilled personnel, and developing a capacity for honest and impartial judgment all require the attention of agency leaders, as does communication of these strengths to the general public.[62]

Conflict of Interest: The Keating Five Scandal

The second case is very different. In 1987, Charles Keating, a financier and owner of the Lincoln Savings and Loan institution, had engaged in a few questionable practices that had caught the attention of suspicious regulators. The well-connected Keating asked five senators to meet with him to see what, if anything, might be done on his behalf. That he had contributed various amounts of money to their election campaigns was, we may safely assume, not an irrelevant considerations in the senators' decision to at least hear him out and perhaps do even more to lend assistance. A few of them did go further. Though none of the five completely escaped criticism, Alan Cranston, a Democrat from California, was eventually singled out by the Senate Ethics Committee for a formal reprimand – a judgment he unrepentantly disputed.

> There is *no precedent* for the Senate disciplining a Senator for actions such as mine. The Senate *never* has determined that it is an ethics violation for a Senator to engage in legitimate constituent service on behalf of a contributor because it was – or might appear to be – close in time to a lawful contribution to a Senator's campaign or to a lawful donation to a charity that the Senator supports .... There is a *fundamental difference* between a Senator acting on behalf of a constituent and a Senator acting for his personal gain. It is one thing to say that a Senator should not do anything in his official capacity that appears to bring him personal gain. It is quite another to say he should not do anything in his official capacity that appears to benefit supporters or contributors. The former is a conflict of interest and a violation of the public trust. The latter is not only

not a violation of trust, but a fulfillment of it. Its appearance can be improper only to those who distrust the system itself.[63] [emphasis in original text of pre-pared remarks]

Was this a routine case of public officials fulfilling their duty to represent a faithful constituent as fairly, legally, and vigorously as possible? Or was it the kind of violation of democratic precepts that diminishes the sometimes-frag-ile faith of citizens in their government? On the one hand, bribes do violate the trust we place in leaders. They are private benefits given to a public offi-cial at the expense of the public good – benefits the official could receive only by virtue of the access, power and influence that comes with his public posi-tion. Campaign donations, on the other hand, are a normal and sanctioned part of the political process, and the legitimacy of the system that currently exists depends upon being able to distinguish between proper and improper ex-changes. When bargains and quid pro quos are everyday grist for the political mill, it surely does shake faith in the system if virtually every mutually ben-eficial act is considered suspect.

Yet there was something troublesome about this incident. As a commen-tary at the time suggested, it had 'come to symbolize public distrust of elected officials.' Identifying precisely which actions crossed the line and why is not as easy as it first appears, however. It requires a very carefully drawn set of distinctions.

In his own analysis of this case, Dennis Thompson has provided more than a few. He considers the Keating Five scandal a case of 'mediated corruption,' a concept he develops to account for those acts that subvert the democratic process even though the public official receives no direct personal gain and violates no law. Thompson explains, 'The corrupt acts are mediated by the political process. The public official's contribution to the corruption is filtered through various practices that are otherwise legitimate and may even be du-ties of the office.'[64] In other words, the gains and benefits received by the politician and the constituent may not themselves be improper, but if the pro-cess of making the exchange runs counter to broader democratic principles, the offense is no less real. Thompson suggests that acts of mediated corrup-tion are increasingly likely in the complex processes of democracy that have evolved where, despite ever more codified rules and regulations about mat-ters such as conflicts of interest, compensation for outside activities, and many other activities, so much remains uncertain and provisional. Such acts will also be harder to classify as corrupt 'unless we make moral judgments about the kind of democratic processes we wish to encourage ... [We] should not suppose that we can understand corruption without making value judgments about politics.'[65] If we object to certain acts because they subvert the democratic process, we need to be clear which features of the democratic process need protection and why.

First, what did the Senators do on behalf of Keating that caused such concern? Thompson, who served as a consultant to the Senate Ethics Committee, offers this account drawn from the committee's report and the extensive hearings. In 1987, Keating was a prominent financier active in promoting deregulation of the savings and loan industry. Specifically, he opposed laws and regulations limiting direct investment by savings and loans institutions. Edwin Gray was head of the regulatory board that administered those regulations objectionable to Keating. According to Thompson, Gray became Keating's most persistent target. Gray also had launched an investigation of Keating's Lincoln Savings and Loan – an institution that two years later would, in fact, collapse in dramatic fashion with losses even far greater than many of the other savings and loan that failed during the crisis. But that vindication of the regulators' suspicions would come later and gets us ahead of the story.

Keating was well known to the five senators: Cranston from California, DeConcini and McCain, both from Arizona, Riegle from Michigan, and Glenn from Ohio. He had filled their campaign coffers with a combined total of $1.3 million. On the evening of April 2, 1987, the senators met with Gray in DeConcini's office and asked him why the investigation of their 'friend' was taking so long. Gray later said he felt intimidated, but at the end of the meeting he suggested the senators meet directly with the examiners in San Francisco. Shortly thereafter, they did and told the examiners they considered this a case of a government agency harassing a constituent. The examiners responded that they were about to make a criminal referral. After that meeting, Senators Riegle, Glenn, and McCain backed off, perhaps realizing that matters were more complicated than they first imagined, but DeConcini and Cranston continued their intercessions.

Cranston's defense rested on the claim that what he did on behalf of Keating was indistinguishable – morally and procedurally – from what other Senators do everyday in various ways for all different kinds of constituents and campaign donors. To accept that claim, as Thompson notes, requires accepting one of two interpretations of political life, neither of which is very satisfying. The competitive politics theory, for example, sees political life as the inevitable and endless clash of individual and group interests. Cranston and Keating's actions were simply part and parcel of a system designed so that aggressively pursued interests and factions would be reined in by equally aggressive but opposing interests and factions. The system would be self-correcting and therefore dependent upon (not resistant to) constituents and representatives doing all that they possibly could to advance their cause. Elected officials not only may go to bat on behalf of a constituent; they are obligated to do so. Cranston did what anyone else in a similar situation would and should do. It was not corrupt but part of a competitive, stable, interest-based system.[66]

The other view of politics that allows Cranston to deflect criticism is the pervasive corruption theory. Everybody acts as Cranston and Keating did, and that is not virtuous by any means, but the problem is with the corrupt system itself not the individuals within it. Apart from the empirical question whether everyone in the system does in fact operate in a similar fashion, the theoretical perspective that politics is inherently corrupting invites cynicism of the cruelest sort, for it is pointless to try to distinguish ethical from unethical behavior if all politics by definition is ultimately corrupt.[67] It is clear, however, that neither the competitive politics theory nor the pervasive corruption theory leaves room for trust as a factor in leadership. Under the former, political actors compete on the basis of interest and cooperate strategically rather than on the basis of trust. Under the latter, mistrust is the foundation in a system where trust becomes a liability, in effect rendering those who do trust at a severe disadvantage in public life.

To find fault with Cranston's intercessions and hold him accountable therefore calls for a different view of politics, one in which different principles of political life hold sway. Thompson does construct a set of reasons why the Keating Five scandal 'goes to the heart of the problem of trust.' A review of at least a few of them provides not only a coda to the Keating Five case. It serves as a wide-angle lens, taking in many of the principles of leadership and democracy discussed to this point, and underscoring the basic proposition: judging how a leader has fulfilled his responsibility and duty requires endorsing a particular perspective on democracy.

First, Cranston's acts violated the democratic process because of an inconsistency between private actions and publicly stated positions, thus making it more difficult for his constituents – specifically those who elected him – to hold him accountable. Cranston was a generally liberal, pro-choice, advocate of activist government and regulated financial markets. Keating was the mirror image on virtually every major issue. Though he had certainly had every legal right to contribute to Cranston's campaign despite these fundamental disagreements on public issues, and although Cranston violated no law by looking into the regulatory action being taken against a citizen, the mutually beneficial arrangement in this political arena was, as Thompson points out, apolitical. Consistency between positions taken on public policy issues and acts taken on behalf of an individual constituent speak to the integrity of the officeholder. Inconsistency jeopardizes trust because the voter is unsure whether the publicly stated position is genuine. And in a democratic system that values public justification for political acts, Cranston could find no justification other than he would do the same for any other citizen, invoking an axiom perilously close to an attorney's claim that everyone deserves his day in court, that a representative should advocate for a constituent without making judgment on the merits of the claim.

But, of course, the defense that Cranston was providing Keating with the same service as anyone else is suspect. Even though his actions apparently violated no law, and even though senators do routinely perform what has come to be known as 'constituency work,' the active, persistent, and personal involvement on Cranston's part was not routine. It is not the case, of course, that each of Cranston's several million constituents could possibly receive an equal amount of his time and attention. It does not make any sense to deny a constituent a service on the grounds that it is more than would be granted to the amount of service rendered to the least well-served constituent. But when the filter for determining who receives differential treatment is so clearly a financial one, then constituents without comparable financial resources find their trust in the system diminished. To be sure, charges of 'appearance' of favorable treatment should not be casually leveled, since appearance can too often be in the eye of a less than disinterested observer. But the magnitude of Keating's financial support, especially in light of his strong policy disagreements with Cranston, should have made the senator more sensitive to his constituents' reactions.

The point is more significant, however, than merely 'it looks bad for the senator.' Such apparent favoritism in a democratic system that places a priority on fairness and equality does jeopardize trust more broadly. Recall John Locke's admonition that leaders gain trust when they exercise discretion for the public good and not for the unfair advantage of one interest over another. Private citizen Keating had privileged access to the corridors of public power for reasons that seemed to have little to do with the merits of his claim. Rather, his ticket was one unavailable to the vast majority of citizens Cranston represents. A fixed star in the constellation of liberal democracies is the prevention of the abuse of public institutions for private purposes.[68] In this case, political power converged with economic power in a manner that seemed to grant one citizen unequal treatment.[69]

The relationship between trust and democratic leadership is more intricate than we realize, in no small part because democracy in the modern administrative state is more complex than we realize and we have not yet come to terms with it. The good news is that the evolution of institutional forms, like evolution in the biological world, fulfills certain needs.[70] In a liberal democracy, political and administrative structures are not merely bureaucratic delivery systems for services set up only in response to citizens' demands and interests. Each piece may have been separately designed, but when they come together, they form a kind of collage with two dominant motifs blending into each other even as they remain distinct: the protection of individual liberty contrasting with attempts to coerce individuals through laws and other means to engage in collective action. In a typical statement of the problem, Stephen Holmes explains,

> Time consuming proceduralism is the price citizens pay for liberty. Such exasperating delays provide an indispensable chance for reconsidering legal principles, double-checking facts, correcting first impressions, and cooling turbulent emotions. Legal snags and hurdles help irrational and biased creatures to be somewhat less irrational and biased when deploying the full force of a state to crush an individual's life.[71]

Holmes was speaking of legal proceedings but the same might be said for political proceedings as well. Achieving collective action must be done within a severely constrained institutional environment.

This movement to ever-increasing social complexity is pervasive and so inexorable that we seem unaware of it and all its implications. One of those implications has been the theme of this chapter. Political trust must be distinguished from personal trust, because inevitably the trust we place in political leaders is partly our trust in the institutions they direct. That depersonalizes trust. In so doing, it robs trust of some of its virtuous and even romantic characteristics. It also diminishes the lofty rhetoric sometimes used to describe the personal and emotional relationships between leaders and followers. But it is a more grounded version better suited to the social complexity we cannot reverse and the liberal democratic principles we have fashioned to cope with it.

This not a cause for lament, as I detect it is in the writings of such stalwarts as James MacGregor Burns. In his seminal work on leadership, he describes with typical insight (but I think misplaced concern) the plight of 'institution-bound policymakers.' They are:

> ... susceptible to pressures that would reduce their role to that of mere agent of the narrow and short-run purposes that engage most administrators, high and low ... They concentrate on method, technique, and mechanisms rather than on broader ends and purposes ... They transact more than they administer, compromise more than they command, institutionalize more than they initiate. They fragment and morselize policy issues ...[72]

All true, I suppose, but also unavoidable because of the reasons we have the complex institutions we do. 'Leaders are entangled in collective leadership institutions, administrative, legislative, or judicial that limit their capacity to appeal over the heads of their peers to broader but more remote publics.'[73] Under certain conditions, some might see that as a good thing.

Burns, though, is right in this respect. Political leadership is about ends, purposes and values; and leaders must not become preoccupied with means and short-term demands. That is the theme of the next chapter, at least in some ways. The institutional forms in which leaders find themselves are part of the ends and purposes of a liberal democratic state. Our trust in leaders – our *political* trust – depends substantially on their ability to respond and work towards our collective purposes while demonstrating fidelity to the principles of process embedded in our institutional forms.

Notes

1. Maureen Dowd, 'The $7 Million Man,' *New York Times,* (July 16, 2000), 15 (wk).
2. Mark E. Warren, 'Democratic Theory and Trust,' in Mark E. Warren, ed., *Democracy and Trust* (Cambridge: Cambridge University Press, 1999), 310–345.
3. Francis Fukuyama, *Trust: The Social Virtues and the Creation of Prosperity* (New York: Free Press, 1995), 310.
4. Richard Morin and Don Balz, 'Americans Losing Trust in Each Other and Institutions,' *Washington Post* (January 28, 1996), A1, A6.
5. J. Roland Pennock, *Democractic Political Theory,* Princeton, NJ: Princeton University Press, 1979, 485–487.
6. Kenneth P. Ruscio, 'Trust in the Administrative State,' *Public Administration Review*, 57, 5 (September/October 1997), 454–458. See also Robert Behn, *Rethinking Democratic Accountability* (Washington, DC: Brookings Institution, 2001), especially Chapter 5. He provides an excellent discussion of discretion and trust in public management. Citing Michael Moore's work, he outlines the paradox of public management: the public's expectation of a certain style of management (limited, cautious, and highly constrained) that would be highly ineffective if the public actually got what they were asking for.
7. Joseph J. Ellis, *American Sphinx: The Character of Thomas Jefferson* (New York: Vintage Books, 1998), 361.
8. James L. Sundquist, 'The Crisis of Competence in Our National Government,' *Political Science Quarterly*, 95, 2 (Summer 1980), 186.
9. Joseph S. Nye, Jr., 'Introduction: The Decline of Confidence in Government,' in J.B. Nye, Jr., Philip D. Zelikow, and David C. King, eds., *Why People Don't Trust Government* (Cambridge, MA: Harvard University Press, 1997), 1–18.
10. James Madison, Alexander Hamilton, and John Jay, *The Federalist Papers,* Madison, 'Number 51' (New York: Penguin Books, [1788] 1987), 320.
11. Chester I. Barnard, *The Functions of the Executive* (Cambridge, MA: Harvard University Press, [1938] 1968).
12. Gabriel Josipovici, *On Trust: Art and the Temptations of Suspicion* (New Haven, CT: Yale University Press, 1999), 3.
13. Louis Hartz, *The Liberal Tradition in America* (New York: Harcourt, Brace and Co., 1955).
14. John Locke, *The Second Treatise of Government,* ed. Thomas P. Peardon (Indianapolis, IN: Bobbs-Merrill Company, [1690] 1952), 92, 95.
15. Ibid., 94.
16. Ibid., 71.
17. Ibid., 97.
18. Ibid., 97.
19. Ibid., 98–99.
20. John Dunn, 'The Concept of "Trust" in the Politics of John Locke,' in Richard Rorty, J.B. Schneewind, and Quentin B. Skinner, eds., *Philosophy in History: Essays on The Historiography of Philosophy* (Cambridge: Cambridge University Press, 1984), 298.
21. Ibid., 290.
22. Ibid., 297.
23. Madison, et al., *The Federalist Papers,* Jay, 'Number 64,' 376.

24. Ibid., 380.
25. Quoted in James MacGregor Burns, *Leadership* (New York: Harper and Row, 1978), 149.
26. Ward Just, *Echo House* (New York: Mariner Books, 1997).
27. Peter Berkowitz, 'The Futility of Utility,' *New Republic* (June 5, 2000), 38.
28. William Bianco, *Trust: Representative and Constituents* (Ann Arbor: University of Michigan Press, 1994), 148.
29. James S. Coleman, *Foundations of Social Theory* (Cambridge, MA: Belknap Press, 1990), 99.
30. Francis Fukuyama, *Trust: The Social Virtues* (New York: The Free Press, 1995).
31. Kenneth O. Ruscio, 'Trust, Democracy, and Public Management: A Theoretical Argument,' *Journal of Public Administration Research and Theory*, 6, 3 (July 1996), 461–477.
32. Oliver E. Williamson, 'Calculativeness, Trust, and Economic Organization,' *Journal of Law and Economics*, 36 (April 1993), 486.
33. James G. March and Johan P. Olsen, *Rediscovering Institutions: The Organizational Basis of Politics* (New York: Free Press, 1989), 27–28.
34. Adam Seligman, *The Problem of Trust* (Princeton, NJ: Princeton University Press, 1997), 8.
35. Kenneth P. Ruscio, 'Jay's Pirouette, or Why Political Trust Is Not the Same as Personal Trust,' *Administration & Society*, 31, 5 (November 1999), 639–657.
36. Stephen Breyer, *Breaking the Vicious Circle: Toward Effective Risk Regulation* (Cambridge, MA: Harvard University Press, 1993), 63.
37. *Mistretta* v. *United States*, 488 U.S. 372 (1989).
38. John Hart Ely, *Democracy and Distrust: A Theory of Judicial Review* (Cambridge, MA: Harvard University Press, 1980), 134.
39. Dennis Thompson, 'Bureaucracy and Democracy,' in Graeme Duncan, ed., *Democratic Theory and Practice* (Cambridge: Cambridge University Press, 1983), 250.
40. Locke, *The Second Treatise of Government*, 81.
41. Montesquieu, *The Spirit of the Laws* (Cambridge: Cambridge University Press [1748] 1995).
42. Madison et al., *The Federalist Papers*, Jay, 'Number 64,' 378.
43. At the Appeals Level, the case was decided as *American Trucking Association, Inc., et al.* v. *United States Environmental Protection Agency* (No. 97–1440) and (No. 97–1441), opinion issued May 14, 1999. When presented to the Supreme Court, it was argued as two separate cases, *Browner* v. *American Trucking Association, Inc., et al.* and *American Trucking* v. *Browner* because of cross-filings and the separate pieces of the litigation. By the time the case was decided, a new Director was in place at EPA and the opinion was issued as *Whitman* v. *American Trucking*. See note 59 below.
44. Transcripts of oral arguments of Seth P. Waxman, Edward W. Warren, and Judith L. French (No. 99–1257) and (No. 99–1426). November 7, 2000.
45. *American Trucking, Inc. et al.* v. *EPA*, 175 F. 3d and 195 F. 3d 4.
46. Cass Sunstein, 'Is The Clean Air Act Unconstitutional?,' *Michigan Law Review*, 98 (November 1999), 307.
47. R. Shep Melnick, *Regulation and the Courts: The Case of the Clean Air Act* (Washington, DC: Brookings Institution, 1983), 7.
48. *Panama Refining Company* v. *Ryan*, 293 U.S. 399 (1935).
49. *Schecter Poultry Corporation* v. *United States*, 295 U.S. 495 (1935).
50. *Chevron* v. *National Resources Defense Council*, 467 U.S. 837, 843 (1984).
51. *American Trucking, Inc. et al.* v. *EPA*, 175 F. 3d. Judge Tatel in dissent.
52. The Federal Administrative Procedure Act 60 Stat 237 (1946) has played a large role in this as well. Of course, there is an entire subfield of law – administrative law – devoted in large part to the procedures of the administrative process. 'Arbitrary and capricious' is at the core of these discussions.
53. Theodore J. Lowi, *The End of Liberalism: The Second Republic of the United States*, second edition (New York: W.W. Norton and Company, 1979), 93–94.
54. Ely, *Democracy and Distrust*.
55. Peter H. Aranson, Ernest Gelhorn, and Glen O. Robinson, 'A Theory of Legislative Delegation,' *Cornell Law Review*, 68 (1982), 65.

56. Gary Lawson, 'The Rise and Fall of the Administrative State,' *Harvard Law Review*, 107 (1994), 1233.

57. David Schoenbrod, *Power Without Responsibility: How Congress Abuses the People Through Delegation* (New Haven, CT: Yale University Press, 1993), 20.

58. Ibid., preface.

59. *Whitman v. American Trucking*, 99–1257 and 99–1427. February 27, 2001. Cass R. Sunstein, quoted in Stephen Breyer's concurring opinion, has written extensively on the non-delegation doctrine. He concludes that the non-delegation doctrine is neither dead nor insignificant but that it has been greatly modified to fit present-day realities. Rather than a doctrine, he prefers to think of non-delegation constraints in terms of 'canons,' subject to principled judicial application and not so unsettling to modern government. See his 'Non-delegation Canons,' *University of Chicago Law Review*, 67, 2 (Spring 2000), 315. His argument here, along with his argument in *Michigan Law Review* (see note 46), seems in harmony, at least in general, with the Court's disposition of *Whitman v. American Trucking*.

60. Richard Epstein, 'Through the Smog: What the Court Actually Ruled,' *Wall Street Journal*, 237 (March 1, 2001), A22.

61. Concurring opinion of Clarence Thomas in *Whitman v. American Trucking*, 99–1257 and 99–1427, February 27, 2001.

62. Marc K. Landy, Marc J. Roberts, and Stephen R. Thomas, *The Environmental Protection Agency: Asking the Wrong Questions From Nixon to Clinton* (New York: Oxford University Press, 1994), 9.

63. Senator Cranston Response to Rudman Statement, *Congressional Record* (December 18, 1991) (emphasis in original).

64. Dennis F. Thompson, 'Mediated Corruption: The Case of the Keating Five,' *American Political Science Review*, 87, 2, (June 1993), 369.

65. Ibid, 378.

66. Ibid, 370.

67. Ibid, 371.

68. Stephen Holmes, *The Anatomy of Antiliberalism* (Cambridge, MA: Harvard University Press, 1996), 207.

69. See, for example, Michael Walzer, *Spheres of Justice: A Defense of Pluralism and Equality* (New York: Basic Books, 1983).

70. See, for example, Robert Wright, *Nonzero: The Logic of Human Destiny* (New York: Vintage Books, 2000), 109.

71. Holmes, *The Anatomy of Antiliberalism*, 242.

72. Burns, *Leadership*, 404.

73. Ibid., 406.

4. On Disney, Presidents, and the Problem of the Parts and the Whole

When the Disney Corporation determined that a huge swath of land abutting its highly successful theme park in Florida would not be needed for expansion, it came up with an alternative plan. Why not construct a town? And not just any town but one with all the features that so many people feel had been lost in their sprawling, fragmented, sterile suburban developments?

Celebration, as it came to be known, was to be a model of the New Urbanism – a shining example of how to recapture the intimate closely-knit atmosphere of the old Main Street-oriented villages. Its downtown would have a mix of businesses and a centrally located school. The residential structures would include everything from apartments and condominiums to cottages and small 'estates,' enabling individuals from different income groups to live side by side. Garages would be hidden away in back service alleys, relegating the car – that most private and solitary mode of transportation – out of sight and out of mind. Front porches would once again be the prominent and functional architectural features. Neighbors would greet each other as they strolled past the front yards where children played and parents, freed from the burdens of traffic congestion and time consuming commutes, relaxed in casual conversation. The town would have preserved open spaces, pedestrian walkways, and all the other physical and natural features necessary to sustain a sense of community. When the idea for Celebration first got off the ground in the early 1990s, Disney decided to hold a lottery to select those who would have the first right to buy property. Over five thousand people participated. By 1997, enough houses had been constructed for fifteen hundred people. Eventually, twenty thousand will call it home.[1]

Celebration is an experiment, maybe not in the eyes of those who so confidently planned it, but certainly for those who try to understand the factors that define successful communities. Disney's market niche – if niche is the right word to describe the extent of its reach – is providing consumers with the means to escape from the day-to-day grind of everyday life. Theme parks are not reality. That is their allure. Movies and cartoon characters are fantasies even when they convey those allegorical lessons of 'letting your conscience be your guide' or the 'circle of life.' Could the corporation that prides itself on imagination and wonder use its expertise to establish real communities, with real citizens and real problems?

Early reviews were mixed. The demand for properties was initially strong and remains so. New owners gave stirring testimonials. 'Everyone's so friendly here, it's like the first week of college,' was one typical assessment.[2] Block parties and community events are commonplace apparently. When crime occurs it is genuinely shocking and anomalous news, not just the routine.

But clouds appeared on the horizon. A nasty fight over the school curriculum was the first community-wide dispute, dividing the parents into groups that were labeled the 'positives' and the 'negatives.' Small rebellions took place against the hundreds of specific restrictions on property owners. In defiance of the 'only white curtains visible from the street' rule, red curtains occasionally made an appearance. An apartment dweller left dying plants on the balcony and refused to have his cat de-clawed. Residents differed among themselves how rigidly such rules should be enforced. Some took the position that people knew the conditions when they came to Celebration and therefore had no right to object. Indeed, there is a hundred-page contract (the 'Declaration of Covenants, Conditions, and Restrictions') all new residents must commit to. Refusal to abide by the contract, so the argument goes, harms the community because the scofflaws are free riders taking advantage of the sacrifices being made in the name of the community by those obeying the laws. Others began to worry that a sense of community was becoming a sense of conformity. 'What this town needs is a few drunks,' one complained. A few wanted it both ways. A journalist tells the story of how one day a resident angrily threatened to sue The Celebration Corporation (TCC) for towing his car from a parking lot about to be paved. 'I've had enough of this. I've got pixie dust coming out my ass.' The next week he was equally upset at the Corporation for not reprimanding his neighbor who had illegally parked her car in the alley behind his house.[3]

Perhaps the main concern, though, was the peculiar hope that somehow politics could be removed from a community. There seemed to be an implication that government – with all its nasty fights over differences, with all its inefficient and bureaucratic programs, with all those politicians cutting deals in city councils and town halls – was primarily responsible for the loss of a sense of community elsewhere. Celebration was to be different. It was to be managed, not unlike the theme parks so efficiently and effectively managed right next door. Residents were not citizens but consumers – buyers of a regime where everyone would read the specifications and consent to them before joining. As one enthusiastic newcomer explained,

> I'd rather live in a civil society than a political society. Here we have a contract with TCC that defines our property rights, and we are not frustrated by bureau-

crats with their own agenda. I don't have a contract with politicians ... What we
have is a deconstructing of government, a rollback of politicization. In a civil
society you feel a desire to fit into a community and satisfy your neighbors. In a
political society, under the heavy hand of government, you expect neighbors to
satisfy you.[4]

Another said he was glad to be a consumer rather than a citizen, because
'they' (the corporation) were 'afraid of him as a customer.' One woman put it
slightly differently, 'Disney gives me a sense of security. They will insure a
quality product, and keep property values up.'[5]

It is telling, in a surreal sort of way, that the two books written about
Celebration's formative phases conclude by noting how often the movie *The
Truman Show* is invoked to explain the atmosphere.[6] In that film, the protago-
nist discovers that his life has been a television show and his family and friends
have been nothing more than a supporting cast, in on the scheme from the
beginning. His hometown was merely a stage set, the daily events merely a
script. With Celebration, too, there is something not authentic. The decorative
water tower that serves no purpose other than to bear a sign welcoming visitors to 'Disney's Celebration' is surely one indicator. But more fundamental is
the desire to be rid of political disputes, a chimerical goal to say the least. As
one writer concluded, 'A real community is messy, ever-changing, and inevitably political – three adjectives that pretty much sum up everything the Disney
culture cannot abide.'[7]

Celebration is a work in progress. It is premature to draw any grand conclusions about its success or failure. But it stands as a peculiar microcosm of
a longstanding theoretical debate about the nature of political life in modern
society. A central, if not *the* central, theme of Western politics is reconciling
individual pursuits with the collective purpose of a community. It manifests
itself in a seemingly endless number of variations: the tension between private and public interest; the yearning for communal bonds in a culture that
values individuality; the debate over whether human nature is inherently selfish or sociable; the conflict between the liberty thought necessary for all people
to reach their potential and the coercion necessary to check the harm that the
exercise of that freedom can sometimes inflict on others; the responsibilities
that come with membership in a community and the rights claimed by citizens; the vitality that diversity brings to a community even as it makes finding
common ground difficult.

Immanuel Kant spoke of the 'unsocial sociability'[8] of humans, their hard-
wired nature that compels them to express their individuality even as they
seek the companionship of their fellow citizens. James Madison spoke of the
danger of faction and the inevitability of like-minded people banding together
to advance their interests in a manner adverse to the common good. He and
others considered balancing liberty with the need for cooperation to be the

main challenge for government. More recently, political theorists have grappled with the 'collective action dilemma' or the systematic manner in which individually rational acts – acts, that is, which advantage the individual – cumulatively disadvantage society.[9]

This chapter develops a proposition. In its simplest form, it is the claim that reconciling the parts with the whole is the fundamental task of political leadership. Others have certainly made that case in various ways. John Gardner has argued, 'We are moving toward a society so intricately organized that the working of the whole system may be halted if one part stops functioning. Thus our capacity to frustrate one another through noncooperation has increased dramatically. The part can hold the system up for ransom.'[10] Though Gardner stresses the currency of the problem, it was in fact recognized long ago and addressed in richly nuanced ways by a number of thinkers. As much as any other proposition, it accounts for the complicated and sometimes-contradictory demands and obligations placed on political leaders. Wrapped up in the proposition are a host of other unsettled claims about human nature, virtue, self-interest, and the public interest. Before we explore those unsettled claims, however, it is necessary to lay some additional groundwork.

If Celebration is a microcosm of the problem of the parts versus the whole, the conditions American presidents face is the problem writ large. In their rhetoric a clear pattern emerges, as a brief and selective sample indicates.

In George Washington's famous farewell address to the nation in 1796, America's first president warned against the divisiveness he saw emerging in the young nation. Federalists, advocates of a strong national government, and those favoring a manufacturing economy were allying themselves against the Republicans, defenders of the states, and advocates for an agricultural economy. Differences about the new country's role in the world were also emerging. Some favored a set of strategic alliances with friendly nations. Others differed on which nations were in fact the friendly ones and on the larger point whether alliances were more entangling than helpful. The fight over who would succeed Washington in the presidency was developing into a bitter electoral contest. Political parties led by ambitious politicians and based on the passions and self-interest of individuals had become a source of great concern to the president.

Washington's address reflected not only his personal thoughts but also the general anxiety of the times. The nation had gone through a painful Revolutionary War, then confronted the failure of the Articles of the Confederation to resolve precisely this question of the parts against the whole, and had just recently ratified an ambitious but still untested Constitution. He and many other Americans were not at all sure the experiment would work. Resurrecting the debate that had so animated the Constitutional Convention eight years before, he acknowledged how difficult it was 'to confine each member of the Society within the limits prescribed by the laws and to maintain all in the secure and tranquil enjoyment of the rights of person and property.'[11] The nature of humanity was the primary cause of the problem. Individuals loved their independence, but that liberty could manifest itself in the destructive pursuit of individual interests. At the same time, it was quite obvious to the president that citizens were mutually dependent on each other. Somehow their interdependence and independence had to be reconciled.

> Let me warn you in the most solemn manner against the baneful effects of the Spirit of Party generally. This spirit, unfortunately, is inseparable from our nature, having its root in the strongest passions of the human mind. It exists under different shapes in all governments, more or less stifled, controuled, or repressed; but in those of the popular form it is seen in its greatest rankness and is truly their worst enemy. The alternate domination of one faction over another, sharpened by the spirit of revenge natural to party dissension, which in different ages and countries has perpetrated the most horrid enormities, is itself a frightful despotism. But this leads at length to more formal and permanent despotism. The disorders and miseries, which result, gradually incline the minds of men to seek security and repose in the absolute power of an individual.[12]

The problem that so consumed Washington's thoughts was the irony that liberty without any recognition of obligations to others would eventually cause citizens to resort to the 'absolute power' of an individual. Washington's advice for avoiding that extreme result was to be ever mindful of common interests, or as he put it, 'the sacred ties which now link together the various parts.' Americans had to establish a common identity based on the 'same religion, Manners, Habits and political principles ... directed by an indissoluble community of Interest as one Nation.' He, at least, would rise above the increasingly strident divisiveness. He offered his thoughts as the 'disinterested warnings of a parting friend, who can possibly have no personal motive to biass [sic] his counsel.'[13]

Washington's farewell address was a clear expression of the problem of the parts and the whole. He located the spirit of factions in the passions of individuals of individuals with conflicting interests. But he warned that liberty itself is lost when the pursuit of private interest overwhelms any sense of the public interest. It was the first president's primary concern for the future of his country. It became not only his theme but also the theme of many of his successors.

One of those successors was Jimmy Carter. In his 1981 Farewell Address, Carter approached the same subject in terms appropriate for his day and age. He had just lost a closely fought election to Ronald Reagan. His presidency had been a series of challenges: the Iran Hostage crisis, the twin economic scourges of inflation and high unemployment, and the energy crisis precipitated by the restrictions on oil shipments from the countries in the OPEC cartel. America's confidence in government was at its nadir. Political writers and commentators had started to speak critically of the 'special interests.' Narrowly defined, they were the scores of lobbyists and interest groups that seemed to hold disproportionate influence in the corridors of Washington's policy-making bodies. Broadly defined, the problem of special interests was the tendency to view all political disputes through the prism of one's own gains and losses. What John Kennedy famously pronounced in his inaugural address twenty years before – 'ask not what your country can do for you, ask what you can do for your country' – now seemed impossibly naïve and politically suicidal.

Like Washington in his day, Carter was greatly concerned about the state of politics. As he exited the stage, he sensed from his vantage point in the presidency that a public interest had to be more than simply the aggregation of everyone's private interests. That public interest was discoverable by means other than each individual simply pressing his or her own preference without concern for others.

> Today as people have become ever more doubtful of the ability of government to deal with our problems, we are increasingly drawn to single-issue groups and special interest organizations to ensure that whatever else happens our own personal views and our own private interests are protected. This is a distinguishing feature in American political life. It tends to distort our purposes because the national interest is not always the sum of single or special interests. We are Americans together – and we must not forget that the common good is our common interest and our individual responsibility. Because of the fragmented pressures of special interests, it's very important that the office of the president be a strong one, and that its constitutional authority be preserved. The president is the only elected official charged with the primary responsibility of representing all the people. In the moments of decision, after the different and conflicting views have been aired, it is the president who then must speak to the nation and for the nation.[14]

For Carter, the public interest was greater than the sum of its parts, and it was the president's responsibility to weave the separate threads together into a seamless fabric.

Twenty years later, Carter joined former Presidents Clinton and Bush to hear George W. Bush deliver his inaugural address. Bush used the occasion to remind the Americans that despite their differences they have common ties. Those ties do not derive from 'blood or birth.' Instead, 'We are bound by ideals that move us beyond our interests and teach us what it means to be citizens.' According to the new president, the 'public interest depends on private character, on civic duty and family bonds and basic fairness, on uncounted, unhonored acts of decency which give direction to our freedom.' The belief that personal virtue is necessary for achieving the public good has a long and complicated heritage. In Bush's version – which as we will see below is a contested one – a sense of obligation to others must balance the drive for one's own self-advancement. Echoing Washington to some degree, Bush claimed that liberty should not be defined as the maximization of individual choice. A freedom to choose if exercised without the moderating effect of virtue – without, that is, a concern for how one's choices could affect others – was dangerous. 'We find the fullness of life not only in options but in commitments. And we find that children and community are the commitments that set us free.' Then, reaching his rhetorical highpoint, Bush made his contribution to a long line of presidential sermons.

> I ask you to seek a common good beyond your comfort; to defend needed reforms against easy attacks; to serve your nation, beginning with your neighbor. I ask you to be citizens: citizens, not spectators; citizens, not subjects; responsible citizens, building communities of service and a nation of character. Americans are generous and strong and decent, not because we believe in ourselves, but because we hold beliefs beyond ourselves.[15]

Bush's inaugural address played to almost unanimously favorable reviews, the only criticism coming from those who wondered whether his policies would match his ideals. But the basic sentiment was warmly embraced. Like his predecessors, he struck a chord that has long resonated with Americans: the belief that in the midst of the diversity, the search for common ground is a noble endeavor. Citizens elevate themselves from their base interests when they join with others.

Few commentators took notice, however, that the greatest applause line in the speech was Bush's pledge to 'reduce taxes' and to give back to the people the money that was theirs and not the government's. The audience voiced their approval loudly and vigorously. It was a revealing moment, for it demonstrated as clearly as one could imagine the inherent tension in a political culture that glorifies, on the one hand, self-sacrifice on behalf of the community while condoning, on the other hand, the unfettered pursuit of one's own advantage. Bush was only the latest leader to appeal to both sentiments without drawing attention to the contradiction. But it is not surprising. The conflict goes back to a time well before America came on the scene. It has a long history.

Notes

1. Michael Pollan, 'Town-Building is No Mickey Mouse Operation,' *New York Times Magazine* (December 14, 1997), 58.
2. Ibid., 58.
3. Andrew Ross, *The Celebration Chronicles: Life, Liberty, and the Pursuit of Property Value*

in Disney's New Town (New York: Ballantine Books, 1999), 325.

4. Ibid., 233.
5. Pollan, 'Town-Building,' 78.
6. Ross, *The Celebration Chronicles*, and Douglas Frantz and Catherine Collins, *Celebration, U.S.A.: Living in Disney's Brave New Town* (New York: Henry Holt and Company, 1999). This discussion draws from the material in both books.
7. Pollan, 'Town-Building,' 58.
8. Immanuel Kant, 'Idea for a Universal History from a Cosmopolitan Point of View,' in Ernst Behler, ed., *Philosophical Writings* (New York: Continuum, 1986), 252.
9. There is also a vast literature in economics that demonstrates in mathematical terms how the individual preferences of voters are imperfectly converted into collective choices. See the seminal work, Kenneth Arrow, *Social Choice and Individual Values* (New York: Wiley, 1963). For a recent variation on this theme, see Donald G. Saari and Katie K. Sieberg, 'The Sum of the Parts Can Violate the Whole,' *American Political Science Review*, 95, 2 (June 2001), 415–433. Arrow's theorem is straightforward. The latest work is not for the mathematically-challenged.
10. John W. Gardner, *On Leadership* (New York: Free Press, 1990), 95.
11. George Washington, *Writings*, Library of America, ed. John Rhodehamel (New York: Literary Classics of the United States, 1997), 969.
12. Ibid., 970.
13. Ibid., 964.
14. Jimmy Carter, 'Administration of Jimmy Carter: Farewell Address to the Nation,' *Public Papers of the Presidents, 1980–1981*, Vol. III, (GPO, 1982), 2889–2893.
15. George Bush, Jr., 'Inaugural Address,' *Weekly Compilation of Presidential Documents*, 37, 4 (January 29, 2001).

5. Public and Private Interest:
The Development of an Idea

Hardly any observation about political or economic society qualifies as a universally accepted law, with perhaps one exception: development and progress lead inevitably to greater complexity. That does not mean there is agreement on what is meant by complexity nor is there agreement on the implications. Sociologists emphasize group and communal interaction, economists the production and distribution of goods and services, political scientists the sophistication of laws and institutions. Adam Smith, the Scottish Enlightenment political economist, noted that social progress occurs linearly in four stages: hunting, grazing, agricultural, and manufacturing, each calling upon ever-greater levels of social interaction and specialization.[1] Robert Wright provides a contemporary variation on the same theme:

> The trend that had gotten humanity to the verge of civilization – bands getting big enough to qualify as villages, which then got bigger and more complex and combined to form chiefdoms – continued. The chiefdoms' villages evolved into something more like towns, which themselves got bigger and more complex ... So there you have it: ancient history in a nutshell: onward and upward, to higher levels of complexity.[2]

Even natural and physical scientists in recent times have attempted to make sense of social complexity with approaches such as chaos theory and evolutionary psychology, the former with its elaborate mathematical calculations of reverberating effects of minute changes and the latter with its explanations of how certain behavioral traits arise in order to help a species (humans included) adapt better to their environment.[3]

To posit complexity, however, is only the first step. The next step is what to make of it. Intuitively, it seems, more parts interacting with each other raises the probability of disorder or at least makes collective action more difficult. Cooperation seems more necessary, the potential pay-off greater, but conflict more inevitable. How will these increasingly complex societies maintain order and bring the parts together for their mutual benefit? If the definition of leadership is collectively purposeful action, as James MacGregor Burns claims, then the leadership dilemma also increases.[4] Collective action itself is problematic, even more so if it must be motivated by a collective purpose.

The story, in other words, is also one of a transformation in the meaning of political leadership – the changed perceptions of leaders, their presumed functions, their responsibilities and obligations. Leaders have come to be portrayed less as mystical hero-statesmen and more as individuals performing a well-defined, institutionally bound set of tasks and duties. To be sure, that could be interpreted as diminishing political leadership, a reduction in its role in society. But it can also be seen as only adding to the challenge of political leadership, its tasks becoming more complex in a manner corresponding to the increased complexity in society. When the statesman had purview over the whole of society, recognizing the common good amidst the parts was not difficult, since there were fewer recognizable parts. When the parts multiplied, finding the common ground became all the more difficult.

The first signs of the shift in thinking occurred during the Renaissance. Church, state, and commerce, previously viewed as an integrated whole, now were increasingly seen as distinct parts of society. Sometimes the separation was dramatic, episodic and revolutionary. Other times it was far more gradual and evolutionary. Commerce in particular acquired a respectable and dignified patina. Historians tell the tale of how the pursuit of wealth, material goods, and prosperity came to be honored as source of virtue and mutual benefit rather than condemned as promoting only the vices of selfishness and acquisitiveness. One explanation was simply the recognition that commerce, especially trade between localities and nations, each with its own expertise and particular advantages, could enhance the prospects of all participants. One person's gain could also be another's. Exchanges between merchants and buyers when they were free to bargain were by definition mutually beneficial. As travel became fundamental to commerce and the territorial reach of buyers and sellers expanded, people of different backgrounds and interests interacted. That necessitated new rules of conduct. Manners, trust among strangers, and reputations now mattered more than before. The norm of civility made its first appearance.

The late Sir John Hale, the British historian, employed the art of the times to illustrate the changing views. For example, he refers to the title page of a 1564 publication of the Nuremberg charter and legal code that depicts a figure of a woman (Respublica) representing the body of citizens and their government. One of her hands points upwards to God. The other rests on the shoulder of Liberality (Liberalitas) representing the wise use of money. Liberality holds a purse in the form of a hive into which coins are dropped from a swarm of industrious and productive bees. Justice (Justicia) and Peace (Pax) are also depicted as figures, both resting contentedly knowing that the individual pursuit of wealth will serve them well. Another example: in a 1460 tableau, Mercury, the god of commerce, makes one of his many appearances in the artwork of the times. In this scene, Mercury and Philogia (Learning) join forces to triumph over the figures representing ignorance and barbarism. An intricate 1585 woodcut, *The Allegory of Commerce*, provides yet another example. Mercury appears once again, this time in flight emerging from a zodiac and carrying the scales of debit and credit. Ably assisted by the figures representing prudence, integrity, and honesty, he watches over countless other figures engaged in transactions of various sorts.[5]

Across the European continent, artists, writers, and statesmen were beginning to find a connection between the advancement of society and the business of buying and selling for personal gain. Commerce in harmony with other parts of society elevated rather than debased the human condition. It was not without its vices or risks. Those would have to be dealt with by justice and balanced by opposing forces. But it did have its advantages, and it could provide a set of virtues to those who made it their profession.

There were implications for political society and for political leaders. If commerce was now a separate entity from the state and the Church, and if some virtuous behavior arose from commercial interactions, and if commerce itself provided benefits for society that the church and state could not, then the role of political leaders would become circumscribed and defined more specifically. It was not diminished. On the contrary, it took on some new roles, even as its sphere became more distinct from others. For one thing, the virtues associated with commerce – civility being the prime example – could not by themselves compensate adequately for the vices of greed and avarice still associated with the pursuit of wealth. There were still the 'passions' that would corrupt society. Those had to be checked in some manner. Second, if there were an increasing number of distinct parts in society, those somehow still had to be balanced against each other. The state would not wither away, and political leadership was never shunted to the background. To the contrary, the state, especially now that it was separate from the church, was arguably more pivotal and political leaders qua political leaders more central.

This time of transition was thus noteworthy for several shifts in social and political thought. Church, state and commerce came to be seen as distinct parts of society, each serving an important function and purpose, each having its distinct vices. With commerce, greed and selfishness of individuals would lead inevitably to the monetization of relationships among individuals. With politics, the drive for power fueled by ambition would lead to a corrupt regime and corrupt rulers. The danger came to be seen as this: if one sector became predominant, presumably the vices of that sector would also dominate. The solution emerged slowly and gradually: a line of thought emphasizing balance among the parts, the vices inherent in each sector counteracting the vices of the other. The problem of the parts and the whole was to be resolved from an engineering frame of mind. How can the many independent parts be made to work in harmony with each other? How can the parts be combined to produce progress? And what was the responsibility of the ruler?

The Enlightenment

The Enlightenment was a period of intellectual creativity lasting one hundred plus years, generally considered to have begun around 1680 and ending in the late 1700s. It is a mark of its influence on contemporary politics and economics that we barely realize anymore how original and innovative a period it was. Though there have certainly been challenges to the philosophies that emerged during that time, the thoughts of Adam Smith, Francis Hutcheson, David Hume, and John Locke, all from the English and Scottish branch, and those of Diderot, Voltaire, Rousseau, and Montesquieu, from the French branch, still frame the terms of discourse. With their faith in progress, their skepticism about religion, and their reliance on human reason and rationality, these writers redefined how we view society, the state, and economic markets. The individual became the primary unit of society. Liberty and equality became touchstones. Political power, though still viewed as necessary, was also seen as inevitably coercive and therefore a threat to liberty. The 'towering achievement' of the Enlightenment philosophers, according to Burns:

> ... was the application of their intellectual resources to one of the most demanding and perplexing problems facing political philosophers seeking to puzzle out the relation between liberty and power. The question concerned the way in which various arrangements for distributing power within governments, combined with certain methods for representing social classes, estates, or other entities in government could best maximize individual liberty without crippling the effectiveness of government in realizing government's fundamental aim, the maintenance of justice and order.[6]

The publication in 1687 of Isaac Newton's *Principia* is one marker for the beginning of the period. Newton's positivism led him to discover basic laws in nature, most famously the assertion that any action or force generates an opposing reaction or force. Specifically, he wrote, 'To any action there is always an opposite and equal reaction; in other words, the actions of two bodies upon each other are always equal and always opposite in direction.'[7] Newton of course had in mind the physics of objects in motion and the energy they generated. But the basic perspective was taken up by others and applied to the dynamics of society. If physical forces caused reactions, could not the same be true of forces in society? Helvetius certainly thought so. 'As the physical world is ruled by the laws of movement so is the moral universe ruled by laws of interest.'[8] A clear proponent of the idea that self-interest motivated every action, he believed that 'sociability is the effect of want ... That the love of men for their brethren is the effect of the necessity of mutual assistance, and of affinity of wants, dependent on their corporeal sensibility, which I regard as the principle of our actions, our virtues, and our vices ....'[9]

The extension of the Newtonian logic to social dynamics went something like this. Individuals had the ability to think for themselves. That enabled them to determine their own interests. But they were also creatures of their passions, often self-interested seekers of their own advantage operating freely to pursue their own version of the good life. On the one hand, the ability of individuals to reason for themselves argued for liberty and freedom. On the other hand, wouldn't the pursuit of individual interest work against the common interest? The problem was how to rein in the passions and self-interest of individuals and achieve a common good without the kind of coercion that could lead to the denial of liberty.

The solution came in various formulations of a basic idea. The interests of individuals would check the interests of other individuals. One force would generate an opposite force. Montesquieu worried about the pernicious effects of ambition in a republic or a monarchy, but drew some comfort from Newtonian logic. 'You could say that it is like the system of the universe, where there is a force constantly repelling all bodies from the center and a force of gravitation attracting them to it. Honor makes all the parts of the body politic move; its very action binds them, and each person works for the common good, believing he works for his individual interests.'[10] The system would achieve equilibrium by correcting itself through its own internal laws of motion. 'Political liberty,' Montesquieu inferred, 'is present only when power is not abused, but it has eternally been observed that any man who has power is led to abuse it; he continues until he finds limits. Who would think it! Even virtue has need of limits. So that one cannot abuse power, power must check power by the arrangement of things.'[11]

The logic attained its most metaphorical extreme in Bernard Mandeville's 1705 *Fable of the Bees*.

> Thus every Part was full of vice,
> Yet the whole Mass a Paradise;
> ...
> Their Crimes conspired to make them Great;
> And Virtue, who from Politicks
> Had learn'd a Thousand Cunning Tricks,
> Was, by their happy Influence,
> Made Friends with Vice; And ever since,
> The Worst of all the Multitude
> Did something for the Common Good.

This was the State's Craft, that maintain'd
The Whole, of which each Part complain'd:
Thus, as in Musick Harmony,
Made Jarrings in the main agree;
Parties directly opposite
Assist each other, as 'twere for Spight;
And Temp'rance with Sobriety
Serve Drunkenness and Gluttony.[12]

In Mandeville's world, the personal vice of avarice would collectively lead to the public good. Even the 'worst of all the multitude' in selfish pursuit of private advantage would be doing 'something for the common good' by checking the selfish pursuits of others. Adam Smith's famous 'invisible hand' also captured the essence of the claim.

> By pursuing his own interest he frequently promotes that of the society more effectually than when he really intends to promote it. I have never known much good done by those who affected to trade for the public good. It is an affectation, indeed, not very common among merchants, and very few words need be employed in dissuading them from it … Without any intervention of law, therefore, the private interests and passions of men naturally lead them to divide and distribute the stock of every society, among all the different employments carried on in it, as nearly as possible in the proportion which is most agreeable to the interest of the whole society.[13]

Now all of these writers, especially the unfortunately caricatured Smith, complicated their thinking about the 'interests and the passions,' as Hirschman so ably explained in his influential analysis of the period. Some left considerable room for traits that enabled people to feel sympathy for the sufferings of others, identify with others less fortunate, and recognize a public good. They posited a basic innate 'moral sense.' Smith's *Theory of Moral Sentiments*, which predated *The Wealth of Nations* and was considered by Smith himself a superior work, claimed that humans naturally feel sympathy for others.[14] There were dissenters to the view that such a sense could be found. Still, for all the differences, a basic idea was taking shape about how to reconcile the parts and the whole. It depended upon balance and self-correction within the system.

Montesquieu

And so we come to Baron Charles Louis De Secondat Montesquieu.

No individual writer can possibly be considered *the* representative of the Enlightenment. There were simply too many variations on the themes. With that point conceded, however, an effective strategy for identifying and explicating the distinctive thought of the times is to dig deeply into one body of work. Montesquieu's *The Spirit of the Laws* is a defensible choice. A long, discursive, disjointed work in many respects, it nevertheless raises the points most critical to our story. Certainly, the problem of the parts and the whole is front and center for Montesquieu. Along the way, we encounter questions of the public good and private interest, the balance among the sectors of society, the evolving forms of the state and commercial markets, and the distinction between political and private virtue. *The Spirit of the Laws* is a classic Enlightenment text – not *the* classic, perhaps, but a central and highly significant text.

It draws us particularly to the leadership issues raised by the Enlightenment thinkers. In an earlier work, *Considerations of the Grandeur of the Romans and the Cause of Their Decline* (1734), Montesquieu telegraphed one of the implications of the shift in thinking. In words reminiscent of Machiavelli's insight into fortune, he reminded us that leaders help societies shape their future. 'It is not chance that rules the world ... There are general causes, moral and physical, which act in every (regime), elevating it, maintaining it, or hurling it to the ground.'[15] Judith Shklar, a political philosopher who wrote on the origins of modern liberalism and was one of the leading interpreters of Montesquieu's work, concluded that his approach 'led him to brush aside that staple of republican history, the great military and political hero. In his history great men were insignificant except at the very beginning of cities. Later they scarcely mattered.'[16] The task of political leadership was de-mystified. Political leaders would influence the fate of their regimes – but not from a lofty perch high above the populace where the proximity to the divine mattered more than their affinity with the people. Instead, they would be in the institutional trenches, working as one part of a multi-faceted society.

Montesquieu's birth in France in 1689 followed the Glorious Revolution in England by just a few short months, a sure sign that he was a child of the Enlightenment. His parents had no financial standing, but Montesquieu secured admission into the nobility in short order. His uncle – his father's oldest brother – had no heirs and gave Montesquieu all the accoutrements necessary for aristocratic status: his title of Baron, extensive land, access to the upper circles of society, and a general sense of membership in the French nobility. A marriage to an heiress and the acquisition of additional land ensured his future not only as a man of letters but also as a wine merchant, land baron, and member of the regional parliament. He traveled widely in his youth and celebrated what was considered then (and probably even now) a liberated life style.

His first published work, the *Persian Letters* (1721), a satire on French society, took the form of letters from France written by two visitors from Persia. A cleverly written piece of literature, it attacked religious oppression and the excesses of the monarchy. In one section the Persian visitor innocently describes the pope as a magician, who can make three into one, make bread that isn't bread and wine that isn't wine. Dangerous and irreverent thoughts to be sure, but increasingly common during the time, at least in the salons of Paris. For all its controversial iconoclasm and fictional lightheartedness, *The Persian Letters*, like the later history of Rome, was a serious commentary on society and the politics of the times.[17]

The Spirit of the Laws, however, is the masterwork. Published in 1748, it is a comparative study of the forms of government – monarchy, aristocracy, and democracy. Montesquieu's method is to convey facts drawn from histories of different countries as well as his own travels. Religion, culture, climate, and size of the regimes are only a few of the variables he took into account to identify general patterns about forms of government and its successes and failures. His use of empirical observation to develop general propositions has led many to consider him the father of modern sociology, and the author has justifiably achieved standing as one of the giants of the period. Still, *The Spirit of the Laws* is a difficult work for the reader and perhaps was so for the author as well. Its scope surely must have overwhelmed him. At the beginning of Book 20, in words meant only for that portion of the analysis but which could stand for the entire effort, he lamented, 'The following material would require more extensive treatment, but the nature of the work does not permit it. I should like to guide on a tranquil river; I am dragged along by a torrent.'[18] So much to report. So much to conclude. As twenty-first-century readers, we must be content to draw out the essential parts, to look at a few of the trees without losing sight of the forest, while still trying to do justice to the entire treatise as Montesquieu pleaded with us to do in the introduction: 'I ask a favor that I fear will not be granted; it is that one not judge by a moment's reading the work of twenty years, that one approve or condemn the book as a whole and not some few sentences.'[19]

To begin, consider Montesquieu's delineation of the boundaries of the political realm. Our post-modern sensibilities have attuned us to the claim that the personal is the political and vice versa. There is no boundary (so this argument goes) between the public and the private. Personal relationships inevitably dissolve into assertions of power in some fashion. Discourse in the public arena, no matter how much rhetorical energy is devoted to claims about larger public purposes and the common good, are unavoidably claims of personal advantage, self-interest and one's identity. A political stance derives from the social, cultural, or biological make-up of the person. Detachment and impartiality are not just unattainable; they are not even ideals. To comprehend the argument I must know who is making it. Where one stands in a political debate depends entirely on where one sits and where one comes from.

Montesquieu had a different take. To be sure, the vernacular was different in eighteenth-century France. The issue was virtue. The longstanding view was that individual virtue was necessary for a healthy polity. One purpose of the state was therefore the promotion and development of individual virtue, or at least the creation of conditions that enabled virtue to flourish. By that reckoning, the political and the personal overlapped to a large degree which is one reason church and state had barely distinguishable boundaries. Montesquieu challenged this notion by redefining virtue in subtle ways, drawing the faintest trace of a line that set off to one side the desirable traits of a citizen and to the other the desirable traits of the good person. The effort begins early in the book with a note that wherever the word 'virtue' appears, the modifier 'political' is always implied. Political virtue is 'not a moral virtue or a Christian virtue' and the 'good man ... is not the Christian good man, but the political good man.'[20] Later, he must remind us again, 'I speak here of political virtue, which is moral virtue in the sense that it points toward the general good, very little about individual moral virtues, and not at all about that virtue which relates to revealed truths.'[21] Thus, virtue for Montesquieu was a virtue in the sense that it led to self-constraint, caused an individual to look beyond himself to the general good, and restrained the individual in his relations with others. But it was political (as opposed to generally moral) in its applicability to the distinctive aspects of political relationships rather than personal ones.[22]

Montesquieu's perspective shows up elsewhere in ways that underscore the full significance of this emerging distinction between the public and private. Laws, for example, are not mores. Both guide our behavior, but the former speak 'to the actions of the citizen,' the latter 'to the actions of the man.' Mores are in turn different from manners because mores govern 'internal' conduct, while manners are concerned with 'external' conduct.[23] The author's meaning is not entirely clear, at least in the specifics, but the general message comes through. There are, he insists, fine distinctions to be made among the kinds of relationships we develop in an increasingly complex society. To merge the codes of conduct that govern our personal and civil relationships with the laws that govern our political ones would no longer suffice. Similarly, 'philosophical liberty' consists in the 'exercise of one's will,' while 'political liberty consists in security or, at least in the opinion one has of one's security.'[24] The restraints on liberty in the public realm ought to be devised with the security of others in mind, so that we are politically free to the extent we do not infringe on the security of other citizens.

What makes Montesquieu's claims so complex is that the distinction between the public and the private enables him to solidify the claim that there is a public interest as well as the private interests of individuals. That is, by distinguishing between the public and the private, he constructs a path to another claim that the public good is not merely some derivative of everyone's private interests. The whole is greater than the sum of its parts. Liberal philosophers, and Montesquieu is surely among the earliest and most influential, are often attacked for an insensitivity to the public good, for being obsessed with individual claims and seeming to claim or claiming outright that a public good is a theoretical impossibility. If individuals are the basic political units of society and each has the capacity to determine a good life on his own terms, then how can a public good consist of anything other than the arithmetic sum of everyone's individual interests? But Montesquieu repeatedly defines political virtue as attentiveness to something other than merely one's own benefit. We can also look to Montesquieu's discussion of crime for further evidence. When someone commits a crime against an individual, the state can respond by adjudicating the dispute between the individual parties and arranging for the offender to compensate the injured party. But Montesquieu thought there was an additional consideration. Crimes are also offenses against the body politic, and thus there are state interests to take into account. As Stephen Holmes explains, we prosecute theft, assault, and murder as offenses against society, not merely as offenses between private parties. We also establish a system of independent and impartial judges precisely because we wish to separate private considerations from at least these kinds of judgments about the public good.[25]

It is important to note that Montesquieu crafted this distinction between the public and the private without subordinating the public entirely to the private – without, that is, reaching the conclusion of at least a few of his contemporaries that the purpose of politics is solely to accommodate the private desires, preferences and interests of individuals. No, there was a public interest apart from the individual interests; and the purpose of the state (and by extension political leaders) is to enable societies to discern and attain the public interest. To understand how Montesquieu reached that conclusion, it is necessary to put a few more pieces in place, each of which builds upon Montesquieu's theme of balance and moderation in democracies.

Commerce

One piece has to do with his embrace of the world of commerce. He took the Renaissance view and advanced it several steps. The interaction of those engaged in commerce fosters the spirit of 'frugality, economy, moderation, work, wisdom, tranquility, order, and rule.'[26] Ambition and competition are innate in humans, and thus wealth or the prospect of it can only enhance these virtues. Commerce also spreads knowledge throughout the land because it brings together an expanding circle of people for mutual benefit. That leads to greater cooperation among those with different 'mores.' 'Commerce cures destructive prejudices, and it is an almost general rule that everywhere there are gentle mores, there is commerce and that everywhere there is commerce there are gentle mores .... The natural effect of commerce is to lead to peace.'[27] Montesquieu did not overlook the potentially deleterious effects of mercantilism. Excess wealth might be a problem, because it could lead ironically to a degree of comfort that would dilute the acquisitive virtues. Severe inequality was also problematic, because it could create an impression among the disadvantaged that wealth was unattainable for them. Thus, the laws of the land 'must make each poor citizen comfortable enough to be able to work as the others and must bring each rich citizen to a middle level such that he needs to work in order to preserve or acquire.'[28]

No free-market libertarian by any means, Montesquieu believed that commerce actually requires more laws. Buying and selling depend upon an infrastructure: banks, contracts, and forums for the adjudication of disputes, to mention just a few examples. England prohibited the export of wool, mandated that coal be shipped by a certain method, and prohibited the export of horses unless they were gelded. Those laws hampered the individual trader but in a manner that favored commerce in general. 'Liberty of commerce is not a faculty granted to traders to do what they want; this would be the servitude of commerce.'[29] But if the laws favored commerce in general, it was important that they remain neutral towards any particular interest.[30] The passions of individuals – those impulses that come not from one's reason – were the problem. Individual interest, by contrast, was the result of calculation and therefore of one's reason – and thus more predictable and manageable than the unbridled passions. When engaged in commerce, men would be 'in a situation such that, though their passions inspire in them the thought of being wicked, they nevertheless have an interest in not being so.'[31] State neutrality allowed the interests to contest each other on fair terms, so that presumably the arrangement of interests most beneficial to society would emerge on their own through the competitive process.[32]

Government

So would 'the arrangement of things' be the basis for Montesquieu's most celebrated claim that in government the parts should be separated and balanced. The powers of government – legislative, executive, and adjudicatory – should be assigned to their own office. '[It] has eternally been observed that any man who has power is led to abuse it; he continues until he finds limits,' Montesquieu warns his readers.[33] The solution is found in institutional design, not by denying the reality of the ambition of individuals or the inevitability of the abuse of power, but rather by making it impossible 'by the arrangement of things' for the abuse to occur. No single official will hold all the power. The different functions of government will be assigned to different institutions and the interests of those in one part of government would act naturally as a check on the abuse of power in the other parts. Leadership becomes more difficult. To do anything requires the cooperation and acquiescence of others.

But liberty is more likely to survive. His discussion of the Constitution of England contains famous passages such as these:

> When legislative power is united with executive power in a single person or in a single body of the magistracy, there is no liberty, because one can fear that the same monarchy or senate that makes tyrannical laws will execute them tyrannically. Nor is there liberty if the power of judging is not separate from legislative power and from executive power. If it were joined to legislative power, the power over life and liberty of the citizens would be arbitrary, for the judge would be the legislator. If it were joined to executive power, the judge would have the force of oppressor.[34]

The mechanics of the 'arrangement of things' in government follows the same logic as that in commerce, which followed the basic Newtonian logic. Force counteracts force. The solution to the abuse of power is to separate the parts, even multiply the parts, acknowledge the inherent interests and ambitions of each of the parts, and allow them to check each other. They would balance each other. The solution to the liberty/power dilemma is to allow individuals the freedom to pursue their interests, but only within a system that prevented any single interest from seizing control.

The Size of the Republic

There was one hitch to the plan. As republics grew, it would become increasingly difficult to discern and achieve the common good. It is 'sacrificed to a thousand considerations; it is subordinated to exceptions; it depends upon accidents.' In a small republic, however, 'the public good is better felt, better known, lies nearer to each citizen; abuses are less extensive there and consequently less protected.'[35] There are limits to the Newtonian logic when applied to the social version of the problem of the parts and the whole. Too many parts and too many interests lead to disequilibrium – an excessive 'particularization' of interests. Montesquieu addressed the problem in two ways. One was to develop a federal structure or what he called a 'society of societies.' Each separate unit would be small enough that the identification of common interests would not be impossible. By the same token, uniting with others of a similar size would enable confederation to protect itself from external threats. The earliest arguments for a federal structure were appearing.

The other solution was to refine the function of representation. Representatives would be accountable to the people and responsive to their wishes but not in every detail. Their great advantage, according to Montesquieu, is that they can deliberate about public affairs and instruct each other in the orderly forum of the legislature.

The people are not at all appropriate for such discussions; this forms one of the great drawbacks of democracy. It is not necessary that the representatives, who have been generally instructed by those who have chosen them, be instructed about each matter of business in particular .... [It] would produce infinite delays and make each deputy the master of all others, and on the most pressing occasions the whole force of the nation could be checked by a caprice.[36]

Like many of his Enlightenment contemporaries, Montesquieu attempted to reconcile the imperatives of effective government and the potential threat that the exercise of power posed to liberty. To a greater extent than any of the others at the time, he focused on the institutional arrangement of things. Greater complexity in society would be embraced, not resisted, and it meant an additional layer of complexity in the way we govern ourselves. Leadership would lose some of its mystical overtones and some of its sources of power. It is no exaggeration to say that the task of leadership was being redefined in the process, in good part because of the emerging distinction between individual private interest and collective public interest. It was left to the Founders of the American republic to continue that redefinition. They relied on the thoughts of 'great Montesquieu,' no doubt gaining a deeper appreciation of exactly what he meant by being 'dragged along as if in a torrent.'

Notes

1.   Adam Smith, *The Wealth of Nations*, ed. Andrew Skinner (Penguin Books [1776], 1970), 31.
2.   Robert Wright, *Nonzero: The Logic of Human Destiny* (New York: Vintage Books, 2000), 109.
3.   On evolutionary psychology, see the work of Frans De Waal, especially *Good Natured: The Origins of Right and Wrong in Humans and Other Animals* (Cambridge, MA: Harvard University Press, 1997), and Robert Wright, *The Moral Animal: Why We Are the Way We Are: The New Science of Evolutionary Psychology* (New York: Vintage Books, 1994).
4.   James MacGregor Burns, *Leadership* (New York: Harper and Row, 1978), 434.
5.   John Hale, *The Civilization of Europe in the Renaissance* (New York: Atheneum, 1994), 372–380.
6.   Burns, *Leadership*, 150.
7.   Isaac Newton, trans. I. Bernard Cohen and Anne Whitman, *The Principia: Mathematical Principles of Natural Philosophy* (Berkeley: University of California Press, [1687] 1999), 416–417.
8.   Quoted in Albert O. Hirschman, *The Passions and the Interests: Political Arguments for Capitalism before Its Triumph* (Princeton, NJ: Princeton University Press, 1977), 43.
9.   Helvitius, *A Treatise on Man: His Intellectual Faculties and His Education*, ed. William Hooper (London: Vernor, Hood and Sharpe, 1810).
10. Montesquieu, *The Spirit of the Laws* (Cambridge: Cambridge University Press, [1748] 1995), 27.
11. Ibid., 155.
12. Bernard Mandeville, 'Grumbling Hive: or, Knaves, Turn'd Honest,' in Frederick Benjamin Kaye, ed., *The Fable of the Bees: or, Private Vices, Publick Benefits* (Oxford: Clarendon Press, [1705] 1924), 24–25.
13. Adam Smith, *An Inquiry into the Nature and Cause of the Wealth of Nations*, eds. R.H. Campbell, A.S. Skiner and W.B. Todd (Oxford: Clarendon Press, 1976), 456, 630.

14. Hirschman, *The Passions and the Interests*. On Adam Smith in particular, see Charles L. Griswold, Jr., *Adam Smith and the Virtues of Enlightenment* (Cambridge: Cambridge University Press, 1999); Jerry Z. Muller, *Adam Smith in His Time and Ours: Designing the Decent Society* (Princeton, NJ: Princeton University Press, 1993); and Emma Rothschild, *Adam Smith, Condorcet, and Enlightenment* (Cambridge, MA: Harvard University Press, 2001).

15. Quoted in Mark Hulliung, 'Montesquieu, Charles Louis De Secondat,' in Edward Craig, ed., *Routledge Encyclopedia of Philosophy*, Vol. 6 (London: Routledge, 1998), 492.

16. Judith N. Shklar, 'Montesquieu and the New Republicanism,' in Stanley Hoffmann, ed., *Political Thought and Political Thinkers* (Chicago: University of Chicago Press, 1998), 246–247.

17. Biographical information from Hulliung, 'Montesquieu, Charles Louis De Secondat,' 489–494; and Maurice Cranston, 'Montesquieu,' in Paul Edwards, ed., *The Encyclopedia of Philosophy*, Vol. 5 (New York: Macmillan Publishing Co., 1972), 368–371.

18. Montesquieu, *The Spirit of the Laws*, 338.

19. Ibid., xliii.

20. Ibid., xli.

21. Ibid., 25n, 42.

22. For a discussion, see Samuel H. Beer, *To Make a Nation: The Rediscovery of American Federalism* (Cambridge, MA: Belknap Press, 1993), 221–223.

23. Montesquieu, *The Spirit of the Laws*, 317.

24. Ibid., 188.

25. Stephen Holmes, *The Anatomy of Antiliberalism* (Cambridge, MA: Harvard University Press, 1996), 207.

26. Montesquieu, *The Spirit of the Laws*, 48.

27. Ibid., 338.

28. Ibid., 48.

29. Ibid., 345.

30. Ibid., 346.

31. Ibid., 389–390.

32. Stephen Holmes provides an excellent discussion of the distinction between interests and passions and how the former came to be understood as the product of reasoned calculation. See Chapter 2 in *Passions and Constraint: On the Theory of Liberal Democracy* (Chicago: University of Chicago Press, 1995), 42–68.

33. Montesquieu, *The Spirit of the Laws*, 155.

34. Ibid., 157.

35. Ibid., 124.

36. Ibid., 159.

6. Madison's Fears and Aspirations

Montesquieu was the theorist most cited by the founders of the American republic.[1] That proved to be a problem. He gave them two legacies, not entirely consistent with each other, and thus pointed the founders and ultimately the American political system in two directions. To this day, we struggle with the ambiguity, or if ambiguity is too strong a word, the wavering priority we assign to his propositions about government and leadership. It may be the fundamental dilemma of leadership in modern democracy.

The first of Montesquieu's legacies that so influenced the founders was that political virtue was necessary for a modern republic to thrive. His was not the classical, sweepingly moral and personal virtue of the ancients, but rather preferred form of behavior that would foster a 'love of homeland' and a willingness to pursue a common good, even at some sacrifice to one's own well being. This political virtue was specifically tailored to the increasingly complex modern state. It enabled citizens to see beyond themselves and contribute to efforts to improve their communities. Secular institutions – the complex of groups and organizations we have come to call civil society – were perfectly able to develop it on their own without the intervention of the religious institutions of the day. Civility and tolerance were part of the new package. It was, in other words, a prescription for how citizens would need to behave for a republic to work. It was not a prescription for how to lead a moral life.

The second legacy was Montesquieu's emphasis on the 'arrangement of things' as a means for achieving the common good, while balancing the need for political power with the protection of liberty. To guard against the abuse of power – and by 'abuse' Montesquieu meant the infringement of liberty – one source of power had to be checked by another source. Force had to check force. It was safe to assume that those in power would be sorely tempted to advance their own interests in a manner that would not have much to do with any vision of the common good. Just as an engineer had to account for the laws of motion, force, and gravity when designing a building or a machine, so would the designers of governmental institutions have to account for the laws of interest and ambition. If they did, the system would take care of itself. In other words, the system would lead to the common good despite (in fact because of) the self-interested behavior of those who worked within it. Vice – not virtue – would lead to the common good.

Montesquieu clearly believed that the common good was an end of government. What was left unclear was the meaning of the common good and the method for achieving it – and most importantly for our inquiry, the roles, responsibilities, duties, and obligations of political leaders in the enterprise. If Montesquieu's first legacy emphasizing virtue predominates, the search for the common good looks like an exercise in philosophy. It has normative overtones because of its focus on the obligations citizens owe to one another and the importance of virtue (albeit the political, secular variety). The role of leaders is to engage the community in the search for the public good. That might be done deliberatively, perhaps through discussion and debate among wise, reasonable, dispassionate, and above all disinterested representatives motivated by their love of country or justice. Their quest is a prescriptive and substantive one.

If Montesquieu's second legacy emphasizing vice and institutional checks to correct it predominates, the quest is of a much different nature. The problem, like an engineer's, is not a normative one. It is the application of political 'laws' to the process of politics.[2] The common good emerges not by persuasion and deliberation among disinterested leaders, but rather by bargaining and compromises among interested parties. Here, leaders are obligated to aggressively pursue their particular interests and the particular interests of those they represent. 'The arrangement of things' – the checks and the balances activated by the design of the institutions – serves as the primary protection, not the virtue of the leaders.

A lot is at stake. The dual legacy shapes modern-day views of politics. Montesquieu alone is not responsible for it but he did have an enormous influence on James Madison, the 'father of the Constitution' and the author of several of the most significant Federalist Papers. And nowhere is the valiant effort to reconcile the two perspectives more evident than in some of the key passages written by Madison and repeatedly emphasized by commentators over the years. It oversimplifies matters to assert that Madisonian scholars break into two camps, each emphasizing the way in which one of Montesquieu's themes prevails over the other in Madison's writings. Still, the complexity of Madison's thought has produced some startlingly different interpretations, especially with respect to this problem of reconciling the parts and the whole and achieving the common good.

The claim here is that our modern-day confusion about political leadership is traceable to Madison whose own thinking was traceable back to Montesquieu. That is not to blame Madison, or to criticize him, or accuse him of contradictions. He was the most astute and subtle thinker during a time when the competition for such a designation was as high as it has ever been. But where one stands on how to interpret Madison determines where one stands on the purpose of government and the duties of political leaders. The stakes are indeed high.

The only way to sort out this intricate problem is to go directly to Madison's own words. But to get a sense of the challenge before us, consider first the contest that has emerged among current scholars. The somewhat standard view is that Madison and the Federalists, in general, were the modernists, the forward thinkers who understood the mixed motivations that drove people to political action and who saw the need for careful institutional design as the way to grant government power while minimizing the risk of loss of liberty. As Isaac Kramnick puts it, the Federalists were defined in part by those who opposed them. The 'nostalgic' anti-Federalists objected to the centralization of government because it weakened the direct connections between representatives and their constituents, which in turn jeopardized the sense of community they so cherished.[3] According to this interpretation of the era, the Federalists were the institutionalists, giving some lip service to the need for virtue but in the end resigned to the inevitability of self-interest and the damage it could do to the commonweal. They devised an elaborate system of checks and balances and pinned their hopes on a federal structure and the separation of powers.

But Gordon Wood, the eminent historian of the American Founding, tells an entirely different story. In his view, the Federalists seemed to place a greater emphasis on wise and virtuous leaders who could rise above the emerging sectional and partisan disputes, engage in reasoned and careful debate, and separate whatever personal interests they had from a broader public interest. The Federalists were the nostalgic ones, blithely placing their faith in a model of political leadership out of touch with the reality of how people actually behaved.

> Is it possible that all those original, bold, and farsighted Federalists had their eyes not on what was coming, but on what was passing? Perhaps the roles of the participants in the contest over the Constitution in 1787–1788 ought to be reversed. If either side in the conflict over the Constitution stood for modernity, perhaps it was the Anti-Federalists. They and not the Federalists, may have been the real harbingers of the moral and political world we know – the liberal, democratic, commercially advanced world of individual pursuits of happiness.[4]

Fearful of the pursuit of self-interest increasingly on display in the growing commercial sector during the Founding period, the Federalists (in Wood's version) endorsed a system of government that ultimately relied upon the disinterested, reasoned, goodwill of the leaders. The Anti-Federalists saw that as hopelessly naïve. Leaders were indeed self-interested. They were after all human, and the check upon their self-interest was to keep them in close contact with their constituents, hold them directly accountable, and remove them from office if they proved incapable of fighting on behalf of those who elected them. Madison's scheme to centralize government would lead not to reasoned deliberation but a remote aristocracy comprised of fallible humans no better able than anyone else to separate their own self-interest from the public positions they advocated. Interest not disinterestedness would drive politics. Because the Anti-Federalists saw the world as it is, not as it should be, Wood considers them the better prognosticators of how political life would evolve.

James MacGregor Burns tells yet another version of the story. Like Wood, Burns faults Madison for being obsessed with interests and their potential for thwarting the common good. Unlike Wood, Burns takes Madison to task for relying too much on an institutional answer to the problem and not enough on the wisdom of the people and the initiative of their leaders. Madison over-engineered the structure of government and encumbered it with an elaborate and intricate machine so successful in preventing the takeover by any particular interest that it also frustrated the popular will at every turn. 'Deadlock' was the inevitable consequence. Madison's solution created a problem perhaps even worse than the one it was trying to solve. Angered and disillusioned by the government constantly blocking their preferences, the people would turn away from the political system as a means to better their lives and communities. In effect, according to Burns, Madison institutionalized the interest-seeking behavior of politicians and citizens and made it a self-fulfilling prophecy. Citizens had little choice but to act in a self-interested manner. Madison did not emphasize the importance of virtue in political leaders, as Wood believes; in Burns's view he over-emphasized the 'arrangement of things' and was indeed the modernist – regrettably so.[5]

So which is it? Does Madison's government depend upon reasoned leadership, disinterestedly searching for the public good, removed a step or two from the people but still operating with their well-being in mind? Or does he see leadership as the aggressive pursuit of interest? Does the public good emerge from the arrangement of things or the political virtue of leaders and citizens? Is the threat of any single interest predominating over the public good mitigated not by the wisdom and reason of the leaders themselves but rather by the design of the government – interest checking interest, force checking force, until equilibrium is established?

Madison's thought becomes coherent only if we understand that he had a fear as well as an aspiration. The fear was that particular interests, motivated by their desire to prevail over other interests at their expense, would indeed frustrate the attainment of a public good. Human nature was not altogether benevolent, as experience had shown. And if government was foolishly designed with an assumption of benevolence rather than an assumption of self-interest, the meek and generous would not inherit the machinery of government. They would be trampled by the less generous and more opportunistic. The interests had to be checked and the 'arrangement of things' was the most effective means of doing so. It worked and it preserved liberty.

But if we leave Madison at that point – if we interpret him only through the fears he expressed – we quickly create a caricature of what he proposed. There is a strand of contemporary social thought that plays to this caricature and constructs elaborate models of human behavior based on the premise of single-minded pursuit of self-interest. (I am thinking here mainly of the economistically driven rational choice theory.) But Madison would have had trouble with the one-dimensionality of such an approach. His discussion of the darker side of human nature was only part of his story. He held on to an aspiration, a hope and belief that reason joined with wisdom would eventually discern the true interest of the people. His arrangement of things was designed to pit force against force, to be sure. But it was also designed to create a situation that raised the odds of effective deliberation and understanding among citizens and leaders with different interests and values.

The aspiration – like any aspiration – would not always materialize. The reach would usually exceed the grasp. 'Enlightened statesmen' would not always be at the helm and politics would often fall short of the public good. And so the auxiliary precautions of checks and balances would be necessary and certainly prudent. But Madison was unwilling to abandon the aspiration merely because it would be rarely attained and only with a great deal of difficulty. He imagined a better form of politics, even as he knew he was describing a hope more than a prediction. Some of Madison's interpreters have reached this conclusion. Speaking of the *The Federalist Papers* as a whole (but focusing on Madison), Garry Wills observes that the writers 'can talk of human nature as needing political safeguards, without precluding the high degree of public virtue needed to create and maintain a republic.'[6] James Q. Wilson, no intellectual or political soul mate of Wills by any means, finds that Madison's political man 'is sufficiently self-interested and calculating to make checks and balances necessary but sufficiently virtuous and deliberative as to make it possible to design and operate a constitution that supplies and maintains that system of restraints.'[7]

The Fear

In 1785, the Virginia legislature debated a bill that would levy a tax to support the Christian ministers of all denominations. James Madison, then a member of the legislature, considered it a bad idea. In the young representative's view, the bill would threaten freedom by supporting one faith. Man had reason, which he used to form a conscience; and state endorsement of a particular church, even in such a small and indirect way, amounted to a coercive influence over the thoughts of citizens of other faiths. It was treacherous road to travel. 'Who does not see,' Madison asked, 'that the same authority which can establish Christianity, in exclusion of all other Religions, may establish with the same ease any particular sect of Christians, in exclusion of all other Sects?'[8] If government with all its potential coercive power was getting into the business of choosing one religion over another, each denomination would see the government as either friend or foe. The competition would be fierce (because the prize would be securing the valuable alliance with government) and someone might actually win. When that happened – when one religion held the upper hand in a society – moderation and harmony are sacrificed. 'Torrents of blood have been spilt in the old world, by vain attempts of the secular arm, to extinguish Religious discord, by proscribing all difference in religious opinion.'[9] Government, Madison insisted, would have to be neutral in this contest.

The state of Virginia had two options. It could attempt to impose order and stability on this cacophony of religious beliefs by favoring one religion over another. Or it could reach the same result by letting the sects compete among themselves for the minds, hearts and souls of their congregations. Madison preferred the latter. Let the denominations proliferate. Leave them free to promote their beliefs, neither supported nor encumbered by government policy. 'Every relaxation of narrow and rigorous policy, wherever it has been tried, has been found to assuage the disease. The American Theatre has exhibited proofs that equal and compleat liberty, if it does not wholly eradicate it, sufficiently destroys its malignant influence on the health and property of the State.'[10] In one of his first public writings, Madison thus revealed the rudiments of a logic that would eventually emerge full blown just a few short years later in his defense of the proposed Constitution. As he hinted at the time in a letter to George Washington on a different subject, 'The great desideratum which has not yet been found for Republican Governments, seems to be some disinterested and dispassionate umpire in disputes between passions and interests in the State.'[11] And as he wrote later addressing yet another issue, 'The great desideratum in Government is such a modification of the Sovereignty as will render it sufficiently neutral between the different interests and factions, to controul one part of the Society from invading the rights of another, and at the same time sufficiently controuled itself, from setting up an interest adverse to the whole society.'[12] The parts would continuously compete against each other, thereby preventing any one of them from gaining control; and government would stand apart from the competition, favoring no outcome over another.

Madison's argument against the support of the Christian ministry carried the day and set the stage for a different debate one year later when the same legislature took up the Virginia Statute for Religious Freedom. Though Jefferson was its primary author, Madison was responsible in good part for its passage.

The argument echoed his:

> Truth is great and will prevail if left to herself; that she is the proper and sufficient antagonist to error, and has nothing to fear from the conflict unless by human interposition disarmed of her natural weapons, free argument and debate; errors ceasing to be dangerous when it permitted freely to contradict them.[13]

An even bigger issue loomed on the horizon. In 1787, it was increasingly apparent to Madison and others that the Articles of Confederation were an insufficient governing structure for the new country. The states were each going their own separate ways, forming alliances with foreign countries, writing laws for commerce and manufacturing, even establishing their own currencies. The parts were clearly in ascendance, operating in a fashion that 'is certainly adverse to the spirit of the Union.'[14] Madison once again put pen to paper. The laws were too numerous, he opined, always in flux, too parochial and lacking in fundamental justice. The promise of democratic rule by the people was at risk – a prospect he found 'alarming ... because it brings more into question the fundamental principle of republican government, that the majority who rule in such governments are the safest Guardians both of the public good and the private rights.'[15] Things were not working out as planned.

> Complaints are everywhere heard from our most considerate and virtuous citizens, equally the friends of public and private faith and of public and personal liberty, that our governments are too unstable, that the public good is disregarded in the conflicts of rival parties, and that measures are too often decided, not according to the rules of justice and the rights of the minor party, but by the superior force of an interested and overbearing majority ... These must be chiefly, if not wholly, effects of the unsteadiness and injustice with which a factious spirit has tainted our public administration.[16]

In what was to become his standard form of analysis, Madison proceeded to carefully reason his way through the problem. The parts of the political body will naturally attempt to assert themselves against the common good because any general act cannot fall equally upon all its members. Some will benefit more than others, and each part, seeking to avoid paying the costs for someone else's benefit, will protect its own interests. Madison described a version of what economists now call 'the free rider' problem – the inherent tendency of any participant to take advantage of any other participant's sacrifice for the common good. Madison put it this way: 'distrust of the voluntary compliance of each other may prevent the compliance of any, although it should be the latent disposition of all.'[17] All would know the right thing to do, but unless they could be assured that others would also do the right thing, none would willingly play the role of the gullible and the naïve.

Madison was crafting a political psychology that drew from earlier theorists but was grounded in the observations of the actual experiment in self-government he witnessed around him every day. People aggressively pursue their interests. And although we may wish that they would recognize 'a prudent regard to their own good as involved in the general and permanent good of the community' – a recognition, in other words, that their interest meshes with the good of the community – they too often organize themselves into factions by which he meant: 'a number of citizens, whether amounting to a majority or minority of the whole, who are united and actuated by some common impulse of passion, or of interest, adverse to the rights of other citizens, or to the permanent and aggregate interests of the community.'[18] The divisive spirit is 'sown in the nature of man.' It can be inflamed by the trivial as well as the major: 'a zeal for different opinions concerning religion, concerning government ... an attachment to different leaders ambitiously contending for pre-eminence and power ....' Whatever the specific cause, this 'propensity to fall into mutual animosities' renders people 'much more disposed to vex and oppress each other, than to cooperate for their common good.'[19] The American system of government could not achieve the common good, Madison was saying, by relying upon the goodwill of the people.

Neither could the leaders be depended upon to provide a remedy. Madison reasoned that three factors motivate leaders: ambition; personal interest; and the public good. Unfortunately the first two 'are proved by experience to be the most relevant.'[20] And, thus,

> It is vain to say that enlightened statesmen will be able to adjust these clashing interests and render them all subservient to the public good. Enlightened statesmen will not always be at the helm. Nor, in many cases, can such an adjustment be made at all without taking into view indirect and remote considerations, which will rarely prevail over the immediate interest which one party may find in disregarding the rights of another or the good of the whole.[21]

To complicate matters even more, the citizen–leader relationship was subject to exploitation. 'How frequently too will the honest representative be the dupe of a favorite leader, veiling his sophistical arguments with the glowing colours of popular eloquence.'[22] A governmental system based wholly on trust without suspicion – trust in leaders, trust among citizens – was a recipe for failure. The system needed 'auxiliary precautions.'

We thus arrive at Madison's own well-known formulation of the 'arrangement of things.' Consistent with Montesquieu's advice, the distinct functions of government – the legislative, executive, and judicial – would be assigned to their own separate office and arranged so that their inclinations to preserve and expand their power would be checked by the equal and opposing inclinations of the other branches. In politics as in physics a triangular structure with equal sides produces balance and stability by the very nature of its design and the laws governing its dynamic. It is a paradox but a beautifully reasoned one. The nature of man, which compels him to view the world through the lens of his own interest to the detriment of the common good, becomes the very means for achieving the common good.

> The only answer that can be given is that as all these exterior provisions are found to be inadequate the defect must be supplied, by so contriving the interior structure of the government as that its several constituent parts may, by their mutual relations, be the means of keeping each other in their proper places ... Ambition must be made to counteract ambition. The interest of the man must be connected with the constitutional rights of the place ... This policy of supplying, by opposite and rival interests, the defect of better motives, might be traced through the whole system of human affairs, private as well as public. We see it particularly displayed in all the subordinate distributions of power, where the constant aim is to divide and arrange the several offices in such a manner as that each may be a check on the other – that the private interest of every individual may be a sentinel over the public rights.[23]

Madison's other structural solution, though consistent with this logic, departed from Montesquieu in its application. In *The Spirit of the Laws*, Montesquieu concluded that small republics were better able to achieve a common good because of the greater likelihood of mutual interests and the ease with which the community could deliberate and resolve differences. Troubled by the intemperate behavior of the states that Madison saw all around him and faced with the prospect of a rapidly expanding republic with a multitude of interests, Madison reasoned his way to a different conclusion. In the matter of 'whether small or extensive republics are most favorable to the election of proper guardians of the public weal ... it is clearly decided in favor of the latter ....'[24]

> Extend the sphere and you take in a greater variety of parties and interests; you make it less probable that a majority of the whole will have a common motive to invade the rights of other citizens; or if such a common motive exists, it will be more difficult for all who feel it to discover their own strength and to act in unison with each other. Besides other impediments, it may be remarked that, where there is a consciousness of unjust or dishonorable purposes, communication is always checked by distrust in proportion to the number whose concurrence is necessary.[25]

Unquestionably, Madison had a skeptical view of human nature. Unquestionably, he devised a solution to the problem of the parts and the whole not by relying upon a change in human nature but by fighting fire with fire, designing a governmental system that converted (he hoped) the self-interest into a public interest. If that were the only message of Madison's story, however, we would be left with a dismal depiction of the responsibilities of leaders. They would be obligated to do not much more than aggressively assert their interests all along the way, never having to worry about the larger picture, confident that the system would churn out the public interest without any leaders having to worry about it.

But that was not all that Madison had to say. The expectations were greater. 'The aim of every political constitution is, or ought to be, first to obtain for rulers men who possess most wisdom to discern, and most virtue to pursue, the common good of the society; and in the next place, to take the most effectual precautions for keeping them virtuous whilst they continue to hold their public trust.'[26] Madison had greater things in mind for those in positions of responsibility, even as he designed a system knowing that we would often get something less.

The Aspiration

Madison and Thomas Jefferson were friends, fellow Virginians, contemporaries who shared the bond that could only come from the challenges they faced together during extraordinary times. But they did not always agree. Jefferson, the imaginative, idealistic, and sometimes imprudent thinker would fire off eloquent and provocative letters to Madison (and others), invariably provoking a polite rebuttal objecting to Jefferson's poorly developed sense of practicality. One particular disagreement was whether 'frequent appeals to the people' on matters of governance were prudent. Jefferson opened the debate while he was in France on the eve of its infamous Revolution that happened to coincide roughly with the drafting of the Constitution in America. The effect of being in a country where a true revolutionary zeal was reaching its zenith while his own country was wrestling with the aftermath of a somewhat differently motivated upheaval must have been disorienting to Jefferson. It led to one of his most analyzed missives and one of Madison's most effective responses.

Jefferson claimed that 'the earth belonged to the living' and that nothing done by current generations could be or should be binding on future generations. He was speaking mainly of financial debts. It was irresponsible and unjust to incur debts that would allow the current generations to live better if it meant imposing the costs on descendants. Jefferson looked first at the injustice of private debts and then expanded his argument to public debts. But his logic drove him even further. If he was right about the financial obligations passed from one generation to another, could not the same be said about legal and constitutional arrangements? How could a system of laws passed by one generation bind another? Shouldn't future generations be able to re-write Constitutions? Frequent appeals to the people – every nineteen years, every generation, if necessary – would not only be legitimate but necessary.[27]

Madison immediately saw the problem. On the specific matter of financial debt, he rejected Jefferson's claim as actually constricting the ability of present generations to improve the lot of their descendants, for debt could be used to the benefit of those who come later; and therefore at least some portion of the cost could justifiably be placed upon them. The American Revolution resulted in an enormous financial burden for the new country, but surely Jefferson would not agree that those who lived after the break with England were worse off because they had to service a few loans. Borrowing as investment was perfectly legitimate. 'Equity requires it. Mutual good is promoted by it. All that is indispensable in adjusting the account between the dead and the living is to see that the debits against the latter do not exceed the advances made by the former. Few of the incumbrances entailed on Nations would bear a liquidation even on this principle.'[28]

On the larger point, Madison was even more persuasive. Future generations tacitly agreed to the Constitution. With the difficulties of the Constitutional Convention still fresh in his mind – the bitter debates; the painstaking compromises; the need to operate in secrecy; the uncertainty throughout the land as leaders convened and put a halt to everyday business – Madison could only wonder how any country could long endure what would amount to a permanent debate over the structure of its government. 'Would not a Government so often revised become too mutable to retain those prejudices in its favor which antiquity inspires, and which are perhaps a salutary aid to the most rational Government in the most enlightened age? Would not such a periodical revision engender pernicious factions that might not otherwise come into existence?'[29]

Madison's objection to Jefferson's generational argument reveals a particularly shrewd insight. On the one hand, Madison was giving full voice to his skepticism about the ability of the people to engage in continuous deliberation over fundamental matters of governance. The citizenry was collectively too impulsive, too intemperate, and too prone to being swayed by their passions rather than their reason. 'The *passions,* therefore, not the *reason,* of the public would sit in judgment. But it is the reason, alone, of the public, that ought to control and regulate the government. The passions ought to be controlled and regulated by the government.'[30] But – and this is critical – there was at least the capacity for reason. Madison saw his task as arranging the system of government to maximize the probability of reason prevailing over passion. There were a variety of factors to take into account. One was the size of the deliberative body. If it was too large, reasoned debate was hopeless, no matter how enlightened, well-meaning and virtuous the participants. 'In all very numerous assemblies, of whatever characters composed, passion never fails to wrest the scepter from reason. Had every Athenian citizen been a Socrates, every Athenian assembly would still have been a mob.'[31] It was necessary, therefore, to create conditions that would allow calm and dispassionate debate, one that would:

> ... refine and enlarge the public views by passing them through the medium of a chosen body of citizens, whose wisdom may best discern the true interest of their country and whose patriotism and love of justice will be least likely to sacrifice it to temporary or partial considerations. Under such a regulation it may well happen that the public voice, pronounced by the representatives of the people, will be more consonant to the public good than if pronounced by the people themselves, convened for the purpose.[32]

Here was Madison advancing an extremely important claim, one that seemed to come very close to synthesizing the legacies of Montesquieu. The arrangement of things would not only neutralize the vice of self-interest. It would promote the virtue of reason and disinterestedness. If the system could be designed to enable leaders, at times, to separate their own interests from the public interest, to engage in true deliberation, then the people would be well served. The conditions in which deliberation took place determined the behavior of the participants. Along the way towards this claim, however, it is important to note that Madison was allowing for behavior that was not purely self-interested, a concession he made explicit in *Federalist Papers* Number 55:

> As there is a degree of depravity in mankind which requires a certain degree of circumspection and distrust, so there are other qualities in human nature which justify a certain portion of esteem and confidence. Republican government presupposes the existence of these qualities in a higher degree than any other form. Were the pictures which have been drawn by the political jealousy of some among us faithful likenesses of the human character, the inference would be that there is not sufficient virtue among men for self-government; and that nothing less than the chains of despotism can retrain them from destroying and devouring one another.[33]

The issue remains with us today, as we will see, framed in terms that Madison would still recognize. But it is important to remind ourselves at this stage before we make the transition to contemporary democratic theory that this is not a rarefied, esoteric debate. It does go to the heart of how we think leaders do behave, should behave, how we should judge them, and what responsibilities and obligations we impose upon them. Though surely leaders have ambition and personal interests, as Madison believed; and though surely those motivating factors often prevail over the motivation to achieve a public good, should we be so fatalistic that we abandon any hope, any expectation that some leaders will occasionally attempt to rise above their own interest – and actually succeed at doing so?

Without yet venturing too far into the contemporary theories, it is worth mentioning in this context the rather dismal take on such matters offered by the increasingly influential school of rational choice theorists. At its best, rational choice theory provides elegant and insightful models of political behavior – and does indeed seem to provide intriguing explanations for why things turn out the way they do. It has, as social scientists like to say, a lot of 'face validity' when it pronounces on certain aspects of legislative, executive, and judicial behavior, not to mention some forms of voting behavior. At its worst, however, its simplifying assumption about single-minded pursuit of interest gives 'parsimony' a bad name. And it too often shades the distinction between how leaders and citizens do behave and how they should behave. Madison's 'fear' becomes downgraded to a simple matter-of-fact recognition of everyday life we should neither lament or praise but merely view with a cool detachment.

Citizens and leaders do indeed have interests, but simply taking those preferences as givens, without any thought of how they were formed or that they may possibly be changed through persuasion, reduces all political statements to something not much different in kind than consumer impulses in the marketplace. An argument that African-Americans should have equal rights is not the same kind of 'preference' as choosing a Toyota over a Ford. By adopting the assumption that individuals always pursue their interests, and that political positions are only expressions of interests and preferences, rational choice theories seem to set aside a critically important set of political behaviors – not a large sample, perhaps, but cases that involve some of our most important political debates of recent years. It was best expressed to me (in casual and undocumented conversation) by the political theorist Jean Bethke Elshtain who wondered what would have happened if Martin Luther King on the steps of the Lincoln Memorial had proclaimed, 'I have an interest' or 'let me state a preference.' It would surely have mattered less, and those who might argue 'I have a dream' is simply a more dramatic way of asserting an interest miss the point.[34]

We do recognize and fear the capacity for self-interest among citizens and leaders – with good reason. And our institutions are arranged so that the pursuit of advantage by some is offset by the same motivations of others. But there is an aspiration towards something better, which is why Montesquieu spoke of virtue even as he refined its meaning and why Madison argued that republican forms of government do presuppose at least a modicum of regard for others and the community. The solution to the problem of the parts and the whole does not rest entirely on the ingenuity of political engineers to design institutions that will somehow free our leaders from the need to worry about the greater good. According to Samuel Beer, 'Madison takes seriously the notion that there is such a thing as the public interest, constituting a standard by which the action of government and citizens can be judged.'[35] So should we still, despite the fashionable academic theories of the moment. Sidney Verba, who contributed so much to the scholarship on political participation during a long and productive career, concluded that people do have complex motivations for why they engage in political life.

> If one takes seriously – and I think one should – the reasons people give us for writing or calling officials, they add up to some simple facts: people care about what is going on in their community or in the nation; they act to affect the collective decisions made in the name of the community or the nation; sometimes they seek a collective benefit, but usually not; sometimes the collective outcome they seek can be construed as their own self-interest, oftentimes not. They do it because they think about and care about the public good."[36]

Notes

1. Donald S. Lutz, 'The Relative Influence of European Writers on Late Eighteenth Century American Political Thought,' *American Political Science Review*, 78 (1984), 189–198.
2. B.J. Diggs, 'The Common Good or Reason for Political Action,' *Ethics*, 83, 4 (July 1973), 283–293.
3. James Madison, Alexander Hamilton, and John Jay, *The Federalist Papers*, Kramnick, 'Introduction' (New York: Penguin Books [1788], 1987), 11–82.
4. Gordon S. Wood, 'Interests and Disinterestedness in the Making of the Constitution,' in Richard Beeman, Stephen Botein, and Edward C. Carter II, eds., *Beyond Confederation: Origins of the Constitution and American National Identity* (Chapel Hill: University of North Carolina Press, 1987), 70. See also *The Radicalism of the American Revolution* (New York: Alfred A. Knopf, 1992).
5. James MacGregor Burns, *The Deadlock of Democracy: Four Party Politics in America* (Englewood Cliffs, NJ: Prentice-Hall, 1963), 8–23.
6. Garry Wills, *Explaining America: The Federalist* (Garden City, NY: Doubleday and Company, 1981), 192.
7. James Q. Wilson, 'Interests and Deliberation in the American Republic, Or, Why James Madison Would Never Have Received the James Madison Award,' *PS: Political Science and Politics* (December, 1990), 558–562.
8. James Madison, 'Memorial and Remonstrance Against Religious Assessments (1785),' in *Writings*, Library of America, ed. Jack N. Rakove (New York: Literary Classics of the United States, 1999), 31.
9. Ibid., 34.
10. Ibid.
11. James Madison, 'To George Washington, April 16, 1787,' in *Writings*, 81.
12. James Madison, 'Vices of the Political System of the United States (April 1787),' in *Writings*, 79.
13. Thomas Jefferson, 'A Bill for Establishing Religious Freedom (1777, 1779),' in *Writings*, Library of America, ed. Merrill D. Peterson (New York: Literary Classics of the United States, 1984), 347.
14. Madison, 'Vices of the Political System of the United States (April 1787),' 71.
15. Ibid., 75.
16. Madison et al., *The Federalist Papers*, Madison, 'Number 10,' 123.
17. Madison, 'Vices of the Political System of the United States (April 1787),' 73.
18. Ibid., 73; and Madison et al., *The Federalist Papers*, Madison, 'Number 10,' 123.
19. Madison et al., *The Federalist Papers*, Madison, 'Number 10,' 124.
20. Madison, 'Vices of the Political System of the United States (April 1787),' 76.

21. Madison et al., *The Federalist Papers*, Madison, 'Number 10,' 125.
22. Madison, 'Vices of the Political System of the United States (April 1787),' 76.
23. Madison et al., *The Federalist Papers*, Madison, 'Number 51,' 318–20.
24. Madison et al., *The Federalist Papers*, Madison, 'Number 10,' 126–27.
25. Ibid., 127–28.
26. Madison et al., *The Federalist Papers*, Madison, 'Number 57,' 343.
27. Thomas Jefferson, 'Letter to James Madison, September 6, 1789,' in *Writings*, 959–965.
28. Madison, 'To Thomas Jefferson, February 4, 1790,' in *Writings*, 474.
29. Ibid.
30. Madison et al., *The Federalist Papers*, Madison, 'Number 49,' 315.
31. Madison et al., *The Federalist Papers*, Madison, 'Number 55,' 336.
32. Madison et al., *The Federalist Papers*, Madison, 'Number 10,' 126.
33. Madison et al., *The Federalist Papers*, Madison, 'Number 55,' 339.
34. For an example of this critique, see generally, Robert B. Reich, ed., *The Power of Public Ideas* (Cambridge, MA: Harvard University Press, 1990), especially the essays by Gary R. Orren and Steven Kelman.
35. Samuel H. Beer, *To Make A Nation: The Rediscovery of American Federalism* (Cambridge, MA: Belknap Press, 1993), 261.
36. Sidney Verba, 'The 1993 James Madison Award Lecture: The Voice of The People,' *PS: Political Science and Politics* (December 1993), 682.

7. The 'Parts and the Whole' in Contemporary Times

The problem of the parts and the whole – the reconciliation of private and public interest – continues to significantly shape contemporary discussions of democracy and our perceptions of the responsibilities of leaders. Even among liberal political theorists – again remembering that liberal is used here in the broad historical sense – there is considerable disagreement about exactly how to negotiate that reconciliation. That is only fitting, of course, since one of the basic presumptions of liberal regimes is that disagreement is a permanent and inescapable feature of political life, at least when freedom of thought is priority. Contemporary liberal theorists, true to the legacy established by their predecessors, differ on precisely why people disagree; they differ on the prospect for reaching any kind of consensus; they differ on whether it is primarily the economic interests of citizens or their moral values that are the most intractable; and they differ on the most legitimate mechanisms for constructing policy in the face of all this conflict. But what defines them as liberals is the common initial premise that conflict, as unpleasant as it may be, is far preferable to the steps that would be needed to eliminate it entirely. From there, they travel down different paths to arrive eventually at different conclusions about the duties and responsibilities of leaders.

Consider, for example, the position of James MacGregor Burns, who represents what we may refer to the 'common purpose' school of democratic leadership. In Burns's view, leadership of course involves day-to-day struggles with ordinary affairs. But leadership attains a more glorious level when it touches upon the purposes we have in common. At its best, leadership facilitates the process of discerning the points on which we can all agree in the midst of this turmoil. Leaders educate and persuade; they bring citizens to higher levels of awareness about their mutually shared fate. By transforming the way people see the world around them, they effect real and intended change. If leaders take action by force without addressing the motivations and attitudes of followers, they cease by definition to be leaders and become mere wielders of power. The use of power without any attention to the underlying beliefs of citizens may bring about change of some sort but it will not be genuine or lasting.

Paradoxically, it is the exercise of *leadership* rather than that of 'naked power' that can have the most comprehensive and lasting causal influence as measured by real change. This is because leaders engaging with the motivations of followers and of other leaders at all levels of movements and organizations are able to exploit the massed social energies of all the persons consciously involved in a joint effort. There is nothing so power-full, nothing so effective, nothing so causal as common purpose if that purpose informs all levels of a political system. Leadership *mobilizes*, naked power *coerces*. To be sure, leaders, unlike power holders, will have to adjust their purposes in advance to the motive bases of followers, but this still leaves a wide field for leadership, innovation and action. Moreover, unity of purpose and congruence of motivation foster causal influence far down the line. Nothing can substitute for common purpose, focused by competition and combat, and aided by time.[1]

Isaiah Berlin, however, saw it differently:

> ... [It] seems to me that the belief that some single formula can in principle be found whereby all the diverse ends of men can be harmoniously realized is demonstrably false. If, as I believe, the ends of men are many, and not all of them are in principle compatible with each other, then the possibility of conflict – and of tragedy – can never wholly be eliminated from human life, either personal or social. The necessity of choosing between absolute claims is then an inescapable characteristic of the human condition.[2]

Now I do not mean to suggest that Berlin completely dismisses the potential for consensus at some practical level of policymaking; nor does Burns gloss over the messy disputes of democratic life. Both are too subtle, sophisticated, and insightful in their thinking to succumb to such one-dimensional views of democracy. I also do not mean to suggest that they reside on the outer and opposite ends of a 'liberal thought' continuum, Burns holding down the position of 'find-the-common-purpose' and Berlin the position that there are only multiple and irreconcilable ends. But there is surely a difference in emphasis, and a great deal of contemporary democratic thought maneuvers within these different emphases.

The dispute reveals itself in two areas of contemporary democratic thought, each of which has profound implications for leadership theory.

First, the tension between the public and private interests these days is (properly) cast in terms of depicting a political society that consists of 'something more' and 'something less' – something more than isolated, atomistic individuals pursuing only their private preferences without regard to their dependence on and their duties to others; and something less than the communitarian portrait of widely shared norms and values supported by the political order.[3] The formulation echoes – faintly but unmistakably – Madison's hope of finding the true public will and his fear that sometimes, maybe even often, a flawed search would infringe on liberty. John Rawls's concept of 'overlapping consensus' is an example of one contemporary project that takes on the challenge. Amy Gutmann and Dennis Thompson's 'economy of moral disagreement' and legal scholar Cass Sunstein's notion of 'incompletely theorized agreements' are other examples – less well developed, perhaps, than Rawls's but important variations on the same theme. As compatible as these three approaches may be in their overall tendencies, they differ on some key points. One is what precisely leaders should do in the face of disagreement. In matters of deliberation, for example, is it preferable to move up the 'ladder of abstraction' to achieve some agreement on substantive values and principles and arrive at some understanding of a common good? Or is it more prudent and practical to move down the ladder and seek agreement on means and process?

Second, leadership within this terrain – between individualism and community; between private interest and public good – calls upon a fairly specific set of virtues. It cannot simply rely upon the arrangement of things, some well-crafted institutional design that allows leaders and citizens the luxury of doing nothing more than asserting their narrow interest, confident that some invisible hand mechanism will combine those interests to manufacture a common good. Rawls, Gutmann and Thompson, and Sunstein, each in a different way, identify at least a few leadership virtues appropriate to liberal democratic regimes. In line with the thoughts of Montesquieu, and mindful of the caution exercised by liberals when it comes to the sensitive matter of prescribing virtues, they argue that the virtues need to be ones specifically tailored to the political realm – and therefore dependent upon preserving the distinction between the public and the private. These civic virtues would include sympathy for others in different situations, tolerance for differing views, impartiality as a way to understand the distinction between one's self-interest and the public interest, and honesty as a condition for trust.

An illustration of these points is the problem of what Gutmann and Thompson call moral constituency.[4] Moral constituents are individuals not directly represented in a particular jurisdiction but who arguably should be taken into account by the jurisdiction as it decides matters of public policy. Examples of moral constituents include future generations or those who live elsewhere. For a host of reasons, the problem of moral constituency will increasingly frame the leadership challenge in democracies. It has the best chance of being resolved only within the context of the 'something more and something less' approach of contemporary liberalism.

In a society comprised of citizens with very different beliefs and values, how should citizens agree to disagree as they seek a basis for cooperation and mutual support? What are the ground rules? More important, how should citizens behave towards each other when they disagree? What are the responsibilities of leaders and public officials in the face of this disagreement? One line of recent thought comes from a family of theorists committed to achieving mutual respect and greater understanding of the positions of others through democratic deliberation. It is impossible to survey the entire range of positions that fall under this heading, but to gain an appreciation for the key components and how they lead to suggestions for the legitimate role of leaders, we can trace one thread beginning with a fairly specific application to the judiciary, then on to a wider view of democratic institutions in general, and finally to the fully developed positions of John Rawls.

The categories are strained. Strictly speaking, Rawls is not usually considered a deliberative theorist. But like the others he asks how citizens should appropriately behave towards each other when their disagreement is, at least to some extent, the consequence of conflicting principles, beliefs, and value systems as opposed to merely interests and preferences. At a minimum, citizens should treat the positions of other citizens with respect – provided the positions they espouse are at least arguably consistent with the wider democratic values of the society. That is not the same as endorsing the moral positions of others, nor does it imply abandoning one's own moral convictions. But it does call for a democracy that seeks greater understanding among its citizens, a sentiment Rawls shares with deliberative democrats. Both he and the deliberative theorists see citizens as more than mere carriers of self-interest (though they are surely at least partly that) and as less than altruistic, enlightened, and morally infallible angels. Gutmann and Thompson put it this way: 'A deliberative democracy governed by reciprocity flourishes neither in a society of self-centered citizens nor in a society of saints.'[5] Rawls, as we have already seen, is on the same page.

> The reasonable society is neither a society of saints nor a society of the self-centered. It is very much a part of our ordinary human world, not a world we think of much virtue, until we find ourselves without it. Yet the moral power that underlies the capacity to propose, or to endorse, and then to be moved to act from fair terms of cooperation for their own sake is an essential social virtue all the same.[6]

The task, then, is discover that democratic space that lies beyond deliberating merely to negotiate mutual advantage and short of a common good based on moral beliefs that are anything but common. Within that space, what are the obligations and responsibilities of leaders?

The Judiciary and 'Incompletely Theorized Agreements'

The legal scholar Cass Sunstein makes a case for what he calls 'judicial minimalism.'[7] As political policy-making institutions, Sunstein argues, courts have limitations. The information provided to them is incomplete, framed in legalistic and adversarial language, and directly relevant only to the particular dispute brought before them. Courts do not (or at least should not) roam the political landscape, searching for problems to solve. Their policy agenda is passive, shaped by the parties who feel compelled to bring their disputes to the point of adjudication. Moreover, the legitimacy of the courts is based on their impartiality and the independence of the judges who preside. Officers of the court are accountable to democratic processes, of course, but in a form very different from, say, that imposed upon members of a legislature who are subject to frequent reviews by voters, can be removed at the end of a term, and have as a result a great incentive to be very responsive to their electors. A legislative agenda is much more active, mercurial and unstable.

In part because of this contrast between the institutional features of democratic legislatures and decidedly undemocratic courts, Sunstein wants judges to tread carefully when 'dealing with a constitutional issue of high complexity about which many people feel deeply and on which the nation is divided (on moral or other grounds).'[8] When people in a democracy disagree intensely on an issue – for purposes of illustration, think of abortion, affirmative action, the right to die (physician-assisted suicide), or the boundaries of church and state – it is better for judges to rule 'with the constructive use of silence,' leaving room for other political and civic institutions to respond to changed attitudes, new information, and revised preferences. Citizens should have the opportunity to work through their disagreement even though the process of deliberation is difficult and disorderly. They receive benefits from such an ordeal beyond the simple outcome of solving the immediate problem. If nothing else, the stock of political and social capital is replenished for use in future disputes.

Judicial 'maximalism,' as Sunstein defines it, takes the opposite approach. Those who endorse this approach believe courts should decide definitively and clearly; judges must issue unambiguous and precise rules rather than open-ended standards and principles. The fact that an issue comes before the court is a sign of either a delay or failure on the part of other institutions and the court should seize the opportunity to bring some order to the way society will deal with the issues.

Sunstein's 'one case at time' approach is different from the standard way of thinking about judicial activism and restraint. The language can be confusing. Supreme Court Justice Antonin Scalia is often considered a conservative and an advocate of judicial restraint. He believes firmly in the power of states relative to the federal government, for example, and is clearly pro-life, a strong critic of *Roe* v. *Wade* and a persistent critic of the court's unwillingness to definitively remove itself from what he sees entirely as a political matter. But Sunstein persuasively describes Scalia's opinions as those of a maximalist. They reveal a preference for the court to pronounce its position firmly, thoroughly, and in a manner that will avoid constant rehashing of the same topic. Rather than 'one case at a time,' maximalists prefer to deal with an issue once and for all.[9] Justice Sandra Day O'Connor, by contrast, is Sunstein's example of a minimalist. Her opinions frequently attempt to find the narrowest point on which to resolve a dispute, setting aside bigger points of contention when it is not necessary to resolve them or impossible to do so. Though her opinions provide many examples, her abortion decisions are the most well known. As the swing vote on the Court, she refuses to join in overruling *Roe* v. *Wade* but has allowed a number of state laws that restrict access to abortion so long as they do not place an 'undue burden' on women. As a provisional standard rather than a specifically defined rule, the scope of which will be determined 'one case at a time,' the undue burden criterion is an example of minimalist reasoning, an implicit acknowledgment of the moral position of the fetus, even as it falls short of the pure pro-life position, as well as an acknowledgment of a woman's liberty, even as it falls short of the position that *any* burden placed on a pregnant woman considering an abortion is an undue one.[10]

Sunstein's defense of judicial minimalism rests on an underlying principle. In a pluralistic society, where people inevitably disagree, they should be encouraged to confront their differences and understand each other's point of view. Even if they don't reach full agreement, the process will force a discovery of at least a few narrow points on which they can agree. That confrontation, he believes, is a political process that takes time and requires public forums for deliberation. It is not a legal process and judicial forums are not satisfactory venues for exploring the wide range of possible points of disagreement and facilitating that often-messy process of democratic debate. Judges can support the deliberative process but not supplant it, moderating it and ensuring fairness but not abridging it by imposing an outcome based on legalistic criteria.

Sunstein's argument is partly a practical one. On the Supreme Court with its nine justices, a controlling opinion must garner the support of five members. As a justice moves up the ladder of theorizing and abstract reasoning, he or she finds it increasingly difficult to hold on to the support of other justices who might agree with the outcome but not on the full set of complicated principles underlying any one justice's reasoning. Simply to command a majority, a justice may be forced to move down the ladder. Sunstein wants to emphasize 'the possibility of concrete judgments on particular cases, unaccompanied by abstract accounts about what accounts for those judgments. The concrete outcomes are backed not by abstract theories but by unambitious reasoning on which people can converge from diverse foundations, or with uncertainty about appropriate foundations.'[11] The posture of judges should be 'to make it possible to obtain agreement where agreement is possible, and to make it unnecessary to obtain agreement where agreement is impossible.'[12]

Minimalist opinions are what judges *should* issue given their place in a deliberative democracy and what they often *need* to issue, given the structure of the Supreme Court.

The Economy of Moral Disagreement

Beyond the peculiar institutional features of the judiciary, the normative (as opposed to the instrumental and strategic) argument for incompletely theorized agreements is that such a posture in the face of disagreement is consistent with a fundamental view of how we should treat our fellow citizens. It is, in other words, an ethical argument for certain forms of behavior under conditions of living with people who are different and have different beliefs. Its defense rests upon viewing disagreement in a democracy as an opportunity for achieving better understanding and mutual respect among citizens. Such a temperament has legitimacy across the spectrum of democracy, in community town halls, city councils, and legislatures.

This wider view is elegantly presented in Amy Gutmann and Dennis Thompson's discussion of deliberative democracy. As part of their analysis, they recommend seeking a rationale for one's political position that minimizes the rejection of the moral basis for an opposing position – when the policy debate calls upon moral justification and reasoning.[13] To arrive at that conclusion they set forth a series of premises, all based upon a deliberative disposition in a democracy. Citizens who differ with each other on moral grounds should find a way to get along that goes beyond simple coexistence and rises to the level of mutual respect. One way to do that is to find agreement without rejecting the moral positions citizens bring to the table – even when those moral positions are different from ours. Gutmann and Thompson call this an 'economy of moral disagreement.'

As demanding as it may be, it is only one piece of their intricate 'mutual respect' puzzle. Here is how it all fits together. Because individuals have liberty and should have autonomy, they will arrive at different conclusions on the moral aspects of various public policy questions. Simply put, they have different values and beliefs. One response to that claim is to dismiss it. Individuals do not have elaborately developed value systems but they do have mundane interests and preferences, and politics is nothing more than bargaining and negotiating over mutual benefit. We kid ourselves if we think assertions of moral positions in the political arena are anything other than a veneer for specific interests. The result of political debate has nothing to do with moral disagreement and everything to do with citizens getting what they can.

Another response is that moral disagreement does indeed involve the clash of deeply held comprehensive beliefs. Individuals become deeply committed to a moral view of the world and disappointed that the world around them seems to diverge so greatly from their understanding of what should be. Politics is one means to their desired end. When considered in those terms, the problem is that the only satisfactory result from the standpoint of the citizen making the claim is the imposition of that belief on society. If it is right and morally true, how can the adherent be satisfied with anything less?

But Gutmann and Thompson favor a different response – one that allows for the recognition of moral claims while rejecting the claim that public policy is the declaration of the winner. The liberty and autonomy of individuals imposes a requirement on democratic regimes: each individual should receive respect, including respect for the moral belief they bring to political discussions. Gutmann and Thompson ask for more than just toleration. They expect:

> a favorable attitude toward and constructive interaction with, the person with whom one disagrees ... an excellence of character that permits a democracy to flourish in the face of fundamental moral disagreement ... a distinctively deliberative kind of character ... the character of individuals who are morally committed, self-reflective about their commitments, discerning of the difference between respectable and merely tolerable differences of opinion and open to the possibility of changing their minds or modifying their positions ....[14]

Citizens and leaders in their deliberative democracy need to be mindful of how they present their positions and how they regard the positions of others. The first requirement calls for 'civic integrity.' Individuals should be consistent in the principles they espouse regardless of the political position in which they find themselves. When a public official gets elected by attacking his opponent's entrenched incumbency and promises to impose a three-term limit on himself in order to avoid succumbing to the very same dangers of incumbency, only transparent self-interest seems to explain a later decision to run for re-election at the end of his third term. The principle seemed to have been adopted when it was politically expedient and abandoned when it became inconvenient. Civic integrity also requires consistency between speech and action. The thrice-divorced member of Congress who repeatedly lectures the country on the decline in family values and sponsors the 'Family Defense Act' as a remedy to alarming rise in the divorce rate has a credibility problem regardless of the merits of the position he is advocating. 'Integrity of principle' is another part of civic integrity. Gutmann and Thompson argue that public officials need to acknowledge the wider implications of the policies they recommend. The negative example they provide is the representative who, out of respect for fetal life, advocates greater restrictions on abortion but overlooks the impact of such restrictions on programs that provide for the health and welfare of poor children. It is not that advocating a more restrictive policy on abortion necessarily leads to a specific position on policy for child welfare, but it does impose an obligation on the representative to at least acknowledge the potential connection.

If civic integrity shapes the way we present our arguments, 'civic magnanimity' refers to how citizens and leaders should respond to the positions of others. When a citizen makes an argument on principle, others ought to acknowledge the seriousness of the claim rather than trivializing it or denigrating it as politically motivated. Gutmann and Thompson also call for openmindedness, a willingness to reconsider decisions or be persuaded by the arguments of others. That is sometimes a difficult posture to adopt. The advocate for term-limits who so conveniently converted to the principle of 'let the voters decide' at the end of his third term invites skepticism. It is, shall we say, harder to see the merits of the principle when the shift in principle is perfectly symmetrical with the shift in self-interest. And the thrice-divorced representative so concerned about family values at least has some additional explaining to do. Nonetheless, the message itself almost always involves a principle or a moral justification, even in those unfortunate cases where the message carrier is an unlikely poster-child for the cause. The level of the debate invariably improves when the moral force of the argument is acknowledged irrespective of the individual making it. This is more than an admonition to refrain from rejecting an argument on adhominem grounds. It is a positive duty to respond to arguments based on principle with respect and on their merits.[15]

It is in this context that Gutmann and Thompson arrive at the 'economy of moral disagreement.' 'In justifying policies on moral grounds, citizens should seek the rationale that minimizes rejection of the position they oppose.' The authors are quick to note that such a posture, although it does require open-mindedness, is very different from 'compromising one's own moral convictions solely in the interest of agreement.'[16] Nor does it mean endorsing the moral positions held by others. The economy of moral disagreement is, however, the basis for mutual respect. It acknowledges the right and the ability of others to advance arguments as deeply and legitimately held as one's own. It does not always lead to agreement, but it does improve the chances for understanding.

The economy of moral disagreement also does not imply that policy debates should skirt moral justifications in policy debates. On the contrary, it would be a serious misreading of both the economy of moral disagreement as well as Sunstein's incompletely theorized agreement to see them as excuses for avoiding moral argument in the political arena. They do, however, underscore the delicate nature of admitting moral arguments into democratic and pluralistic politics. On the one hand, citizens do base their political positions in part on deeply held views about what it best for society. To view it otherwise is to fall into the position that self-interest and personal advantage are the only basis for political positions or that moral beliefs can be somehow sequestered or bracketed from political positions. On the other hand, Gutmann and Thompson and Sunstein are also warning that when moral beliefs inform political positions and become part of the public debate, 'anything goes' is an insufficient guide to deliberation. The person making the argument and the person hearing it both have responsibilities to each other.

The Limits of the Practical Best

One fundamental question in the midst of all this deliberation is whether the development of the common good requires grounding in some notion of a particular moral good. If it does, some would argue, then it jeopardizes the liberty of those who may hold moral beliefs other than the one underlying the common good. It would also suffer from a definitional inadequacy: it would be 'good' but a particular good not a common one. But if it does *not* require grounding in a particular moral tradition, others would argue, then a very different problem arises. The common good would be more common than good, a kind of lowest denominator devoid of any real substance or depth, thin gruel as a guide for public policy.

As much as any contemporary philosopher, John Rawls has attacked this question. Not surprisingly, he has received an abundance of criticism, for he has perched himself on a very fine edge by offering a vision of a democratic, pluralistic society that is open to the possibility of shared ends even as it protects the distinctive and competing comprehensive beliefs of its citizens. By comprehensive belief, Rawls means religious and philosophical doctrines that include 'conceptions of what is of value in human life, and ideals of personal character, as well as ideas of friendship and of familial and associational relationships, and much else that is to inform our conduct, and in the limit to our life as whole.' They cover 'all recognized values and virtues within one rather precisely articulated system.'[17] It is precisely for this reason that they cannot therefore serve as the basis for the political order in society. The achievement of Rawls's 'political liberalism' is that he can make this claim without abandoning the possibility of shared ends that are more than mere agreements on process, neutral with respect to the policy that emerges. To balance himself on this edge, Rawls calls upon several familiar themes: the distinction between public and private realms; the identification of distinctly political virtues; a moral psychology of cooperation; and (as we have seen in his discussion of 'public reason') a clear specification of what are legitimate bases for arguments presented in the public sphere.

The first step in understanding his position is to examine the claim that a 'political conception' can be freestanding – that is, not dependent on a comprehensive doctrine. For Rawls, the shared principles of politics are distinct from fully developed moral traditions. They apply only to the activities we pursue in political and economic institutions, all of which are established to accomplish a limited set of objectives. These institutions form the 'basic structure' of society, and although individuals need to work out the manner in which the principles governing the basic structure are consistent with their own comprehensive beliefs, the public justification of the political conception must take on a different cast.

> [Its] content is expressed in terms of certain fundamental ideas seen as implicit in the public political culture of a democratic society. This public culture comprises the political institutions of a constitutional regime and the public traditions of their interpretation (including those of the judiciary), as well as the historic texts and documents that are common knowledge.[18]

Political ends, while linked in an individual's mind to his own moral ends, must have a different basis for agreement in the public realm.

> [The] features of a political conception of justice [as opposed to a comprehensive belief] are, first, that it is a moral conception worked out for a specific subject, namely, the basic structure of a constitutional democratic regime; second, that accepting the political conception does not presuppose accepting any particular comprehensive religious, philosophical, or moral doctrine; rather the political conception presents itself as a reasonable conception for the basic structure alone; and third, that it is not formulated in terms of any comprehensive doctrine but in terms of certain fundamental ideas viewed as latent in the public political culture of a democratic society.[19]

Michael Sandel, among others, attacks the moral psychology underlying Rawls's position. He sees it as calling for the impossible, as asking citizens to somehow 'bracket' their fundamental beliefs from their political beliefs and set aside their most important reasons for making a political argument.[20] To some extent, Rawls is vulnerable to the charge. But his case is more complex. When one makes a political claim in a pluralistic society, and when that claim has the potential to impose losses on others, as most political claims do, it is problematic if the justification depends upon moral traditions not understood by those who might suffer the loss. 'Our exercise of political power is proper only when we sincerely believe that the reasons we offer for our political action may reasonably be accepted by other citizens as a justification for those actions.'[21] Rawls does not go so far as to say that political arguments may not be based on comprehensive beliefs, but he is saying that they must be translated in the political arena into language consistent with the 'public political culture.'

But then Rawls must solve the problem of where the shared political culture does in fact come from. How does it develop? Is it more than simple ground rules – a 'modus vivendi' that enables cooperation but prevents any shared purpose with other citizens, any common moral ground? With a number of critical qualifications, Rawls believes that it goes well beyond mere ground rules and elevates society to higher levels of consensus. His explanation hinges upon an idealized social dynamic – a theory of how individuals initially cooperate on basic procedures and practices and then gradually knit together a stable society built on principles of justice. It is important to note that the dynamic he describes is a philosophical argument, 'idealized' in the sense that the steps are part of analytical theory. The explanation is not a sociological or scientific one, even though it does have traces of the Tocquevillian observations that 'habits of the heart' develop from repeatedly successful interactions with others in a community and even though it does seem consistent with more recent observations on the creation of social capital.

For Rawls, it all begins with the formation of basic institutions to solve matters that require the cooperation of those who do not agree with each other (simple pluralism). Citizens soon find the need to discuss matters within a broader context of principles of justice (reasonable pluralism). From there, agreement emerges on even broader political values and how the political institutions support those values (a constitutional consensus). The success of these institutions over time and the relationships that emerge among citizens 'tend to encourage the cooperative virtues of political life: the virtue of reasonableness and a sense of fairness, a spirit of compromise and a readiness to meet others halfway, all of which are connected with the willingness to cooperate with others on political terms that everyone can publicly accept.'[22] Political groups

> ... move out of the narrower circle of their own views and ... develop political conceptions in terms of which they can explain and justify their preferred policies to a wider public so as to put together a majority ... These conceptions provide the common currency of discussion and a deeper basis for explaining the meaning and implications of the principles and policies each group endorses.[23]

Finally, the constitutional consensus expands into an 'overlapping consensus.' It becomes the foundation for a well-ordered society in which people agree on principles of justice and the political and social institutions that support the principles, and understand how to operate within that basic structure of society.

It is important to note two points. One is that Rawls sees societies as gradually moving up the ladder of abstraction, beginning with agreement on everyday practices and then on broader principles. In this respect, he takes a slightly different approach than Sunstein, and, in fact, argues that one way to move up the ladder and achieve a greater understanding within a society of the broader conception is to have judges locate specific disputes in the context of the broader political conception.[24] He also seems to depart from the 'economy of moral disagreement,' at least according to Gutmann and Thompson, who argue that their view would seek respect for differing beliefs as an end in itself, not merely as a means to agreement on the political conception of justice.[25]

The second point is that the overlapping consensus is, for Rawls, his version of social unity based on the fundamental common *aims* of society – not, strictly speaking, the common *good* of society, as he so precisely and carefully notes. The framing of his position in this manner is, in part, a response to his critics who contend that the overlapping consensus – and indeed the whole theory of political liberalism – sets up a society of distinct individuals who cooperate only to pursue their private ends rather than any public common goals. And, in fact, Rawls does rule out thinking of the overlapping consensus as a form of community, if community means a set of shared values derived from a comprehensive moral tradition.[26] The common conception must be political, and it is therefore limited and restrained – admittedly something less than a full notion of community. It is, as Rawls puts it, the 'limit of the practical best.' It depends on the constitutional basic structure of political and economic institutions – which is Rawls's version of the arrangement of things.

But Rawls also argues that it requires something more than individuals pursuing only their own advantage. Political liberalism affirms the 'superiority of certain forms of moral character,' and it encourages 'certain moral virtues.' Leaders and citizens must have virtues; these virtues, however, must be political ones, the kind that apply to the citizen operating within the established political institution, virtues such as civility, tolerance, reasonableness, a sense of fairness, and mutual trust.

> In this way the political virtues must be distinguished from the virtues that characterize ways of life belonging to comprehensive religious and philosophical doctrines, as well as the virtues falling under various associational ideals (the ideals of churches and universities, occupations and vocations, clubs and teams) and of those appropriate to roles in family life and to the relations between individuals.[27]

These political virtues are 'great' virtues for Rawls, indispensable and not mere luxuries for a liberal state, for without them citizens are unable to participate in the activities of democracy; and when citizens withdraw into private life, they leave politics to the powerful or the self-interested. It is not necessary here to venture too much further into the debate that surrounds this claim by Rawls, but it must be noted that his version of liberalism is not the only one criticized for a failed attempt to balance itself on this precarious edge – to claim that certain forms of behavior are essential for a legitimate liberal state while trying to avoid locating the justification for the preferred behaviors in non-political moral traditions.[28] Whether he succeeds or not is less important at this point than to accept that he and other liberals find such an

argument central to the broader argument that citizens and leaders in a plural-
ist democracy have duties and obligations beyond seeking their own advantage. They should endorse a form of politics that recognizes the needs, interests, and beliefs of others.

Moral Constituency

The problem of moral constituency as described by Amy Gutmann and Dennis Thompson moves us away from the theoretical and abstract and into the
concrete world of policy choice.[29] A moral constituent is someone not directly
represented in a political jurisdiction but affected by the decisions made in
that jurisdiction – and therefore, arguably, someone who should be considered in the formation of the policy. Future generations are moral constituents.
Policy choices made today in social insurance, education, the environment,
and overall levels of spending and borrowing have enormous implications for
citizens years from now. Those who live beyond our borders become moral
constituents as well when various actions – an example would be pollution
moving beyond our borders – impose harm on others who have no direct say
in our policy deliberations.

There is no way to address adequately this problem of moral constituency
unless we construct a model of leadership that goes beyond politics as merely
the pursuit of individual advantage. It requires consideration of duties and
responsibilities to others as part of everyday politics. To raise the stakes even
higher, the evolving complexity in modern society ensures that the problem of
moral constituency will be more and more prominent. Alan Wolfe makes the
argument in a slightly different context. 'To be modern,' he observes, 'is to
face the consequences of decisions made by complete strangers while making
decisions that will affect the lives of people one will never know.' He believes
modernity has presented us with a paradox. As the web of interdependence
becomes more complex, our ability to discern our obligations weakens.[30] We
interact with a widening circle of people, but with less understanding of our
responsibilities to each other. The problem of moral constituency is a particular manifestation of this paradox.

Now, it is surely not the case that simply identifying an impact on moral
constituents is by itself grounds for vetoing the decision. Nor does it make
sense to argue that moral constituents and any indirect representation accorded
to them take priority over actual constituents and the direct representation
accorded to them. As Adam Smith wrote long ago, our obligations to those
closest to us are more keenly felt and properly so than our obligations to what
sociologists have come to call 'generalized others.' 'The man who should feel
no more for the death or distress of his own father, or son, than for those of
any other man's father or son, would appear neither a good son nor a good

father. Such unnatural indifference, far from exciting our applause, would incur our highest disapprobation.'[31]

But feeling no sympathy or obligation to distant others, especially when our actions might be the cause of their distress, even indirectly or partially, does seem problematic. The questions are precisely to what extent should moral constituents be considered in the formation of policy, and precisely how to consider them, given that the electoral mechanism by which representatives are chosen provides no clear incentive to do so and, more to the point, actually may inflict penalties for doing so. One of the most convenient responses from representatives to arguments that they need to consider the standing of those they do not directly represent is that those other moral constituents have their own representatives. They need not be twice represented. And if the political institutions work as they should, all people have their voice. But can we rely upon the institutional arrangement of things, confident that the interests of all the affected parties will clash with each other and meld themselves into a policy that reflects the common good? Or do we need to rely upon something more from citizens and leaders when the policies will affect those who simply cannot speak for themselves in the policy-making bodies?

Here's a specific example of the problem – a small but very revealing one. In 1992, Lawrence Summers, a brilliant young economist who would later become secretary of the Treasury during the Clinton administration and then go on to become president of Harvard University, was chief economist for the World Bank. He wrote an internal memo in language unadorned by political and diplomatic qualifiers and intended only to promote discussion among colleagues on a particular point of economic policy. But it became public and its phrasing generated a great deal of controversy. Summers's conclusion was shocking. 'I think the economic logic behind dumping a load of toxic waste in the lowest wage country is impeccable and we should face up to that.' The reasoning went this way. The cost of pollution is lost productivity. We measure that most conveniently and precisely by calculating wages lost through either morbidity (debilitating illness, contraction of disease, and so on) or mortality (early death). In countries where workers are paid less and where the standard of living is low, the costs of pollution (in terms of lost productivity) will therefore also be less.

Suppose then that a wealthier country with a load of toxic waste becomes concerned about the cost that it will impose on its society. The rich country decides to export that load and is willing to pay another country to accept it. According to the strict economic logic, the low-wage country would willingly accept the toxic waste provided the accompanying payment would compensate for the harmful health effects generated by the waste. And since the health effects in the rich country will be more expensive (remember, the lost wages there are higher than in the poor country), it will improve its situation by paying the low-wage country to accept the pollution, just as the low-wage country will consider itself better off taking the payment and the waste. As Summers put it to his fellow economists, 'The demand for a clean environment for aesthetic and health reasons is likely to have very high income elasticity. The concern over an agent that causes a one-in-a-million change in the odds of prostate cancer is obviously going to be much higher in a country where people survive to get prostate cancer than in a country where under-5 mortality is 200 per thousand.'[32] The dumpee and the dumper will both be mutually advantaged as a result of this voluntary exchange. The economic logic *is* impeccable.

But impeccable economic logic is not necessarily an impeccable guide to policy. Though the worldwide relationship of costs to benefits would be improved by the imagined toxic waste exchange, something is bothersome about the basis upon which the costs and benefits would be distributed. If the residents of the less-developed countries are seen as economic actors only – consumers voluntarily entering into exchanges of goods – our concerns are minimal. But if the transaction is not really voluntary (at least in the sense that there was a genuine choice in the matter) or if one of the goods in question is the kind of good whose true value is not easily converted into monetary terms, then our concerns grow. Both complications seem to apply in this case. Though the poor country may not have been blatantly forced or coerced, the imbalance in the bargaining positions seems to depart from the typical 'comparative advantage' trading partners bring to the table, particularly when one of the goods in question – human health – is so closely related to, if not actually, a fundamental human need. The consent given by the poor country is one borne of desperation. Their comparative advantage, so to speak, was their level of poverty and high rate of mortality. The bargaining advantage enjoyed by the rich country seems to be past some threshold of fairness. And because the health of the citizens is so closely tied to human dignity, it is problematic to have to bargain over it in a conventional commercial negotiation.[33]

Should rich countries consider citizens in poor countries as moral constituents as well as economic actors? The difficulty in this case is how non-economic considerations enter into the formation of policy. Imagine, for example, the political debate that might ensue in a rich country's legislature if representatives from a poor country had direct representation and votes. We would expect the non-economic arguments to be raised. They may not carry the day, but they at least could enter the deliberations and be balanced against the arguments of costs and benefits. The practical difficulty, however, is all too obvious. Poor countries are not represented in a rich country's legislature, nor is there necessarily any injustice because they are not. The institutional arrangement of things provides no incentive for the legislator to consider the moral as opposed to the economic status of those outside the jurisdiction. Any attention given to the arguments that might change the status of the citizens in poor countries from mere economic actors to be bargained with to moral constituents to whom a certain duty is owed would therefore depend upon leaders and citizens broadening public discussion to include matters beyond the raw comparisons of interests and mutual advantage only of those directly represented.

The problem of moral constituency is even more acute when policy decisions affect those in the future. What is our duty to citizens not yet born? Obligations to future generations have historically been at the center of many discussions in political philosophy, but they have received renewed attention for a number of reasons, especially the prominence now given to environmental policy. Our consumption of natural resources, the patterns of land use, and the development of technologies that make our lives more convenient, but generate pollution that will persist for quite some time, have forced the international community to consider whether our advances are coming at the expense of our descendants. The principle of sustainability – the proposition that we certainly have the right to better our lives but not in such a way that we worsen the choices facing future generations – is one attempt at devising a workable concept of intergenerational justice.[34] The trade-offs facing those in the future will undoubtedly be different in the particulars than we face now, but they should not in general be made more problematic or constrained. If they are, we have behaved in an unsustainable fashion. We have purchased a better form of life by taking away from those not yet born.

When costs and benefits of a certain action occur at the same time for a particular individual, it is relatively easy to compare them and arrive at a decision. When the benefits and costs are separated by time, the calculation becomes more difficult, but not impossible. People do it all the time. They calculate whether it is worth borrowing to buy a car or saving and investing for a future goal. In decisions such as these, a key factor is the rate at which the individual discounts benefits in the future compared to the present. A dollar spent today is worth more than a dollar spent in the future, but is a dollar spent today worth more than five dollars spent five years from now? It depends a great deal on the individual's 'time preference,' as well as the prevailing discount rates at the time of the decision. Whether quintupling your money over five years is a good investment depends in part on what other choices are available. The point, though, is that we routinely make personal decisions comparing future benefits and costs.

We routinely make those kinds of decisions in public policy as well – although the trade-off is usually less explicit. Policies for global warming, for using parts of the rain forest for economic development, for oil drilling in protected habitats, for keeping the price of energy low, and many, many others usually have embedded in them a judgment about how much we value current benefits over future costs. When the trade-off becomes explicit, it seems unduly harsh. Suppose there is a choice between two policies. One will save one hundred lives today, but result in five hundred deaths in five years. Another will save one thousand lives in five years, but at the cost of one hundred lives today. The selection reveals the rate at which we compare (or 'discount') future lives versus those in our current generation. The discomfort created by phrasing it this way is one reason these trade-offs remain implicit in many policy debates. But they are very real. They are still very real when we extend the time horizon even farther, to three or four generations in the future, and when the projections of harm come in the form of statistical probabilities rather than certainties.

Framing this problem as a matter of intertemporal comparison of costs and benefits actually understates the challenge. While it does improve the standing of future generations by at least accounting for their interests, it leaves them in the category of economic actors only. The only 'obligation' due them is to calculate their supposed interests against ours, and even that is complicated by the choice of a discount rate and the enormous political incentives, given the limited time horizons of elected officials calculating their own electoral interests, to chose a policy that favors current benefits and future costs. Like the problem of moral constituency for those beyond the borders of a jurisdiction, but to an even greater degree, the institutional arrangement of things does not seem to address the problem adequately. Gutmann and Thompson acknowledge the difficulty, and place their hopes on a form of deliberation that 'depends on the capacity of citizens and their representatives to take a moral point of view' and encourages 'representatives to give reasons that transcend the boundaries of electoral constituency.'[35] In other words, they share an aspiration not unlike Madison's: the hope for a political environment that encourages citizens to see beyond immediate interests.

The problem of moral constituency, whether in the form of intergenerational justice or the fairness of actions whose impacts are felt across borders, will continue to vex modern democratic societies. It is a peculiarly contemporary version of the problem of the parts and the whole, because it expands yet again the number of parts under consideration and reveals to us the newly complicated forms of interaction among them. If, as I claimed earlier, the leadership challenge of modern democracies is to reconcile the parts with the whole, to protect the autonomy of individuals even as we identify their obligations to each other, to honor differences even as we search for common ground, then the future will pose the challenge even more sharply. The past provides guidance. But the current conditions, especially the growing problem of moral constituency, call for new interpretations. What does seem clear is that the institutional arrangement of things, as Montesquieu and Madison both seemed to have anticipated, is necessary but insufficient. According to the political theorist William A. Galston, '[The] operation of liberal institutions is affected in important ways by the character of citizens (and leaders), and that at some point, the attenuation of individual virtue will create pathologies with which liberal political contrivances, however technically perfect their design, simply cannot cope.'[36] Only virtue and a sense of moral obligation can cause leaders to account for the needs and interests of those citizens removed by time and distance. Institutional designs work against it. It is only the latest variation of the dilemma of leadership in a modern democracy.

Notes

1. James MacGregor Burns, *Leadership* (New York: Harper and Row, 1978), 439.
2. Isaiah Berlin, 'Two Concepts of Liberty,' in I. Berlin, *The Proper Study of Mankind: An Anthology of Essays* (New York: Farrar, Straus and Giroux, 1998), 239. For interpretations of Berlin's liberalism, see Jonathan Riley, 'Interpreting Berlin's Liberalism,' *American Political Science Review*, 95, 2 (June 2001), 283–295, and Alan Ryan, 'Isaiah Berlin: Political Theory and Liberal Culture,' *Annual Review of Political Science*, 2 (1999), 345–362.
3. For an insightful critique of John Rawls that makes a similar point but develops it in a different direction, see Claudia Mills, '"Not a Mere Modus Vivendi:" The Bases for Allegiance to the Just State,' in Victoria Davion and Clark Wolf, eds., *The Idea of Political Liberalism: Essays on Rawls* (Lanham, MD.: Rowman and Littlefield Publishers, Inc., 2000), 190–203.
4. Amy Gutmann and Dennis Thompson, *Democracy and Disagreement: Why Moral Conflict Cannot Be Avoided in Politics and What Should Be Done about It* (Cambridge, MA: Belknap Press, 1996), 144–164.
5. Ibid., 91.
6. John Rawls, *Political Liberalism* (New York: Columbia University Press, 1996), 54.
7. Cass Sunstein, *One Case at a Time: Judicial Minimalism on the Supreme Court* (Cambridge, MA: Harvard University Press, 1999).
8. Ibid., 5.
9. Ibid., 209–243.
10. Gutmann and Thompson made a similar point about O'Connor's jurisprudence on abortion. See *Democracy and Disagreement*, 87.
11. Sunstein, *One Case at a Time*, 13.
12. Cass Sunstein, 'Agreement without Theory,' in Stephen Macedo, ed., *Deliberative Politics: Essays on Democracy and Disagreement* (New York: Oxford University Press, 1999), 126.
13. Gutmann and Thompson, *Democracy and Disagreement*, 84–85.
14. Ibid., 79–80.
15. Ibid., 79–91.
16. Ibid., 85.
17. Rawls, *Political Liberalism*, 13.
18. Ibid., 14.
19. Ibid., 174–175.
20. See especially Michael J. Sandel, *Democracy's Discontent: America in Search of a Public Philosophy* (Cambridge, MA: Belknap Press, 1996), 55 ff. Also, Sandel, 'Review of Political Liberalism,' *Harvard Law Review*, 107 (1994), 1765–1794 and *Liberalism and the Limits of Justice*, second edition (Cambridge: Cambridge University Press, 1998), 184–218.
21. Rawls, *Political Liberalism*, xlvi.
22. Ibid., 163.
23. Ibid., 165.
24. Sunstein, 'Agreement without Theory,' 133. Sunstein offers the following quote from Rawls to underscore his difference with him: 'We should be prepared to find that the deeper the

conflict, the higher the level of abstraction to which we must ascend to get a clear and uncluttered view of its roots.'

25. Gutmann and Thompson, *Democracy and Disagreement*, 377nn 43, 44.
26. Rawls, *Political Liberalism*, 201. Ronald Dworkin makes the distinction between a metaphysical and a practical community. The former required too much for liberals to accept. The latter, he argues, is more acceptable because of its emphasis on workable rules of cooperation and mutual assistance in the absence of agreement on values. See his 'Liberal Community,' *California Law Review*, 77 (May 1989), 479–504.
27. Rawls, *Political Liberalism*, 195.
28. Examples include Peter Berkowitz, *Virtue and the Making of Modern Liberalism* (Princeton, NJ: Princeton University Press, 1999); Stephen Macedo, *Liberal Virtues: Citizenship, Virtue, and Community in Liberal Constitutionalism* (New York: Clarendon Press, 1990); and William A. Galston, *Liberal Purposes: Goods, Virtues and Diversity in the Liberal State* (Cambridge: Cambridge University Press, 1991).
29. Gutmann and Thompson identify three types of moral constituents – the two mentioned here plus group identity. I depend heavily on their analysis for the foundation, but I build on it differently. See *Democracy and Disagreement*, especially 144–164.
30. Alan Wolfe, *Whose Keeper? Social Science and Moral Obligation* (Berkeley: University of California Press, 1989), 3–5.
31. Adam Smith, *The Theory of Moral Sentiments*, eds. D.D. Raphael and A.L. Macfie (Indianapolis: Liberty Fund [1759] 1984), 142.
32. Lawrence Summers, 'Let Them Eat Pollution,' *The Economist* (February 8, 1992), 66.
33. For a cogent argument on this more general point, see Elizabeth Anderson, *Value in Ethics and Economics* (Cambridge, MA: Harvard University Press, 1993).
34. There is an extensive literature on sustainability, despite its recent origins. For an update, see Alex Farrell and Maureen Hart, 'What Does Sustainability Really Mean? The Search for Useful Indicators,' *Environment*, 40, 9 (November 1998), 4–9, 26–31.
35. Gutmann and Thompson, *Democracy and Disagreement*, 163.
36. Galston, *Liberal Purposes*, 217.

Conclusion: Is Good Politics Bad Leadership?

Democracy is not sustainable if good politics is bad leadership – if, that is, the measures of political success are different from the measures of successful leadership. Those who demonstrate extraordinary leadership should reap the political rewards of re-election, endorsement by citizens and the steady accumulation of authority to act in the name of the public good. But if 'politicians' are perceived to be something other than effective leaders, and if self-interested, deceitful and shortsighted acts rather than the pursuit of the public good are the coin of the political realm, then the system is out of alignment. The mistrust sure to result will cause democracy to collapse from the burden of cynicism and disengagement. In American democracy today, the charge is all too common. There is a deep impression that 'politicians' and genuine 'leaders' are two different breeds. At the very least, the allegation calls for clarification of what we mean by politics, leadership, and political leadership.

We need first to step back.

The two administrations of Thomas Jefferson's presidency ended with mixed reviews. For all his eloquence in capturing the spirit of freedom and liberty that led to the birth of a nation, Jefferson was uncomfortable and clumsy holding the reins of power. It was ironic justice that an individual whose most enduring legacy was the brief for holding leaders accountable found himself in a position where his most exacting principles were put to the test. His presidency was far from a failure. Indeed, contemporary historians rate him among the best (though usually not among the very best) American presidents. But Jefferson the theorist soared to loftier achievement than Jefferson the politician.

The embargo controversy toward the end of his second administration was perhaps the final straw for a man whose temperament seemed better suited for studious reflection than political combat. Opting for a diplomatic rather than a military response to Britain's challenges on the high seas, Jefferson became the target of vicious criticism from the opposition political party. His daily mail was not pleasant.

Thomas Jefferson: You are the damdest fool that God put life into. God dam you.

And another:

> I have agreed to pay four of my friends $400 to shoot you if you don't take off
> the embargo by the 10th of October.[1]

Despite the bitter fights during the American Revolution, the maneuverings of the earliest presidential elections, his rough tenures as Secretary of State and Vice-President, and his seven years in the presidency, Jefferson had never grown accustomed to the intensity of politics and the harshness of debate. He was a seasoned but a reluctant politician who, with disappointment and regret, eventually understood that policy disputes in a democracy inevitably turn personal and criticism of ideas often elides into criticism of those who hold them. And he did take it personally. 'I became of course the butt of everything which reason, ridicule, malice, and falsehood could supply. They have concentrated all their hatred on me, till they have really persuaded themselves that I am the sole source of all their imaginary evils.'[2]

It was soon to end, however, and on March 2, 1809, days before he was to leave office, he wrote to a long-time friend:

> Never did a prisoner, released from his chains, feel such relief as I shall on
> shaking off the shackles of power. Nature intended me for the tranquil pursuits
> of science, by rendering them my supreme delight. But the enormities of the
> times in which I have lived, have forced me to take a part in resisting them, and
> to commit myself to the boisterous oceans of political passion.[3]

He retired to his mountain-top home Monticello to continue work on its symmetrical architecture and tend to its orderly and manicured gardens, far from the daily crucible of bitter political disputes and far above the unavoidable contradictions of democratic leadership.

Jefferson's dilemma is the dilemma of leadership in a democracy.

The very traits and temperament that qualify individuals for democratic leadership – a reluctance to use power, an acknowledgment of its dangers in a free society, a commitment to the limitations on those who hold power – are the very traits and qualities that handicap individuals who hold leadership positions in such a complex and sophisticated system of checks and balances. American democracy particularly, but most western democracies in one fashion or another, have designed positions of political authority in ways that place a premium on the skillful use of persuasion and the effective exercise of the barely discernible sources of power. The *personal* skills of negotiation and coalition building become essential *political* skills where the sources of formal administrative power are so meager. In Jefferson's case, as his biographer Joseph Ellis has noted, it resulted in the practice of 'benign deception' borne of sheer necessity. In our time no less than in Jefferson's, political authority remains 'severely circumscribed and must achieve its ends more covertly.'[4] Democratic leaders must be adept and skillful in the use of informal power, even as they must honestly profess and truly embody unease with pulling the flimsy levers of power available to them.

Jefferson's voluminous record of correspondence in which he bared his soul for all posterity, confessing his now well-known angst over serving in public office and his relief whenever he could escape to his refuge in the Blue Ridge, might cause one to think of him as the exception rather than the rule. But democratic leaders of any success or degree of effectiveness display the same general pattern, albeit in different circumstances and through unique personalities. Abraham Lincoln, whom many consider the paradigm of the transforming leader, the principled man who rose above petty political practices, was 'through and through a politician,' according to his admiring biographer William Lee Miller. He organized campaigns, gave speeches, debated, traded votes, and engaged in all those messy things we associate with the word political. Miller's eloquent and subtle appraisal of Lincoln, the virtuous and ethical leader, captures his mastery of the leadership challenge in a democracy.

> The significance of Lincoln being a lifelong politician, for an appraisal of the conduct of his life, is that he acted within fairly narrow limits of the possible; that the opinion of the great public was one of those limits; that he was not the lone-wolf moral hero but participated with others in collaborative efforts – parties, legislatures, governments; that calculation and compromise were therefore of the essence in his decision and action; that the great object of his and others' joint efforts was to accomplish society-wide goods through the instrument of government .... Having the awareness and doing the deeds that are encompassed by the term 'politician' would be essential to his achievement.[5]

Yet, one hardly thinks of Lincoln as a 'typical politician.' Indeed, Miller's study is a response to scholars who saw in Lincoln's leadership an apolitical quality. It was Lincoln's willingness to use authority within the limits of democratic restraint and in service to the fundamental good of the country that led to his success. He was a good politician, in Miller's estimate, and a good leader by the estimate of most others.

Theodore Roosevelt is another example. Although he did in fact seem more suited to the rough and tumble exchanges of modern democratic life than Lincoln or Jefferson, his highest achievement reflects a more subtle approach. The difficult task of negotiating the treaty between Russia and Japan – the accomplishment that brought the Nobel Peace Prize to his list of honors – was, in Edmund Morris's assessment, the consequence of 'an inexplicable ability to impose his singular charge upon plural power. By sheer force of moral purpose, by clarity of perception, by mastery of detail and benign manipulation of men,' Roosevelt quietly and skillfully accomplished the impossible. He mastered the skills of the politician and possessed the qualities of a moral, transforming leader.[6]

Though biography has its limitations in leadership studies – a single case study cannot be the basis for theory – the judgments of biographers in these particular cases do suggest a pattern. Jefferson's 'benign deception,' Lincoln's 'calculation and compromise,' Roosevelt's 'benign manipulation' – all are terms fraught with connotations typically associated with the least admirable qualities of the 'politician.' Yet, they weave into a richer tapestry. Jefferson's voice proclaiming the moral significance of liberty and equality and Roosevelt's 'sheer force of moral purpose and clarity of perception' become inseparable from their political acts. Lincoln's life is the best example. He became 'a political leader engaged with the deepest moral fundamentals of the nation. He would come to combine with the realism of the politician a new and unwavering moral clarity.'[7]

To explain this interweaving of moral purpose with the means of political action is the enduring challenge of democratic theory. The intricacies do not lend themselves to neat and tidy claims of empirical verification nor to the catchy enumerated 'leadership lessons' so popular in trendy leadership development seminars. Contemporary leadership studies typically goes to one extreme or the other. At times, it emphasizes the political means and depicts leaders as manipulative, untrustworthy politicians. It becomes the study of mechanics without purpose, and analysis of movement without regard to destination. On the other hand, to ignore the 'politics' and emphasize only the pure unadulterated moral end overlooks the moral significance of the democratic process itself – the deeper and broader reasons for holding leaders accountable, for limiting their power, and for asking more of citizens than simply to acquiesce in whatever ends, moral or otherwise, a leader pronounces.

If the course of democratic theory in modern times, from Machiavelli to Rawls, teaches us anything, it is the need for leaders to demonstrate prudence, practicality, and the acceptance of the art of the possible within a context of moral purpose, ethical reasoning, and transforming vision. The standard for effective political leadership requires no less than the intricate weaving together of both perspectives. Neither alone is sufficient, and the dilemma for democratic leadership – and theory – is to aspire to the high standard, while recognizing that only rarely will it be attained and guarding against the damage that will result when it is not.

Notes

1. Quoted in Merrill D. Peterson, *The Jefferson Image in the American Mind* (New York: Oxford University Press, 1960), 904.
2. Ibid., 904.
3. Thomas Jefferson, 'To P.S. Dupont de Nemours,' in *Writings*, Library of America, ed. Merrill D. Peterson (New York: Literary Classics of the United States, 1984), 1203.
4. Joseph J. Ellis, *American Sphinx: The Character of Thomas Jefferson* (New York: Vintage, 1998), 361.
5. William Lee Miller, *Lincoln's Virtues: An Ethical Biography* (New York: Alfred A. Knopf, 2002), 105, 115.
6. Edmund Morris, *Theodore Rex* (New York: Random House, 2001), 414.
7. Miller, *Lincoln's Virtues*, 230.

Bibliography

A. BOOKS

Anderson, Elizabeth, *Value in Ethics and Economics* (Cambridge, MA: Harvard University Press, 1993).

Arrow, Kenneth, *Social Choice and Individual Values* (New York: Wiley, 1963).

Bailey, F.G., *Humbuggery and Manipulation: The Art of Leadership* (Ithaca, NY: Cornell University Press, 1988).

Barber, Benjamin R., *A Passion for Democracy: American Essays* (Princeton: Princeton University Press, 1998.

Barnard, Chester I., *The Functions of the Executive* (Cambridge, MA: Harvard University Press, [1938] 1968).

Beer, Samuel H., *To Make a Nation: The Rediscovery of American Federalism* (Cambridge, MA: Belknap Press, 1993).

Behn, Robert, *Rethinking Democratic Accountability* (Washinton, DC: Brookings Institution, 2001).

Berkowitz, Peter, *Virtue and the Making of Modern Liberalism* (Princeton, NJ: Princeton University Press, 1999).

Bianco, William T., *Trust: Representatives & Constituents* (Ann Arbor: University of Michigan Press, 1994).

Bissinger, Buzz, *A Prayer for the City* (New York: Vintage Press, 1997).

Bok, Sissela, *Lying: Moral Choice in Public and Private Life* (New York: Vintage Books, 1989).

Breyer, Stephen, *Breaking the Vicious Circle: Toward Effective Risk Regulation* (Cambridge, MA: Harvard University Press, 1993).

Burns, James MacGregor, *The Deadlock of Democracy: Four-Party Politics in America* (Englewood Cliffs, NJ: Prentice-Hall, 1963).

Burns, James MacGregor, *Leadership* (New York: Harper & Row, 1978).

Capella, Joseph N. and Kathleen Hall Jamieson, *Spiral of Cynicism: The Press and the Public Good* (New York: Oxford University Press, 1997).

Carter, Stephen, *Civility: Manners, Morals, and the Etiquette of Democracy* (New York: Harper Perennial, 1998).

Coleman, James S., *Foundations of Social Theory* (Cambridge, MA: Belknap Press, 1990).

De Waal, Frans, *Good Natured: The Origins of Right and Wrong in Humans and Other Animals* (Cambridge, MA: Harvard University Press, 1997).

Dionne, E.J., Jr., *Why Americans Hate Politics* (New York: Touchstone, 1991).

Ellis, Joseph J., *American Sphinx: The Character of Thomas Jefferson* (New York: Vintage Books, 1998).

Elshtain, Jean Bethke, *Democracy on Trial* (New York: Basic Books, 1995).

Ely, John Hart, *Democracy and Distrust: A Theory of Judicial Review* (Cambridge, MA: Harvard University Press, 1980).

Frantz, Douglas and Catherine Collins, *Celebration U.S.A.: Living in Disney's Brave New Town* (New York: Henry Holt and Company, 1999).

Fukuyama, Francis, *Trust: The Social Virtues and the Creation of Prosperity* (New York: Free Press, 1995).

Galston, William A., *Liberal Purposes: Goods, Virtues and Diversity in the Liberal State* (Cambridge: Cambridge University Press, 1991).

Gardner, John W., *On Leadership* (New York: Free Press, 1990).

Ginsberg, Benjamin and Martin Shefter, *Politics by Other Means: Politicians, Prosecutors and the Press from Watergate to Whitewater* (New York: Norton Books, 1999).

Griswold, Charles L., Jr., *Adam Smith and the Virtues of Enlightenment* (Cambridge: Cambridge University Press, 1999).

Gutmann, Amy and Dennis Thompson, *Democracy and Disagreement: Why Moral Conflict Cannot Be Avoided in Politics and What Should Be Done about It* (Cambridge, MA: Belknap Press, 1996).

Hale, John, *The Civilization of Europe in the Renaissance* (New York: Atheneum, 1994).

Hartz, Louis, *The Liberal Tradition in America* (New York: Harcourt, Brace and Co., 1955).

Hazlitt, William, *Characters of Shakespeare's Plays* (London: Oxford University Press, 1966).

Helvetius, *A Treatise on Man: His Intellectual Faculties and His Education*, ed. William Hooper (London: Vernor, Hood and Sharpe, 1810).

Hirschman, Albert O., *The Passions and the Interests: Political Arguments for Capitalism before Its Triumph* (Princeton, NJ: Princeton University Press, 1977).

Holmes, Stephen, *The Anatomy of Antiliberalism* (Cambridge, MA: Harvard University Press, 1996).

Holmes, Stephen, *Passions and Constraints: On the Theory of Liberal Democracy* (Chicago: University of Chicago Press, 1995).

Hughes, Richard L., Robert C. Ginnett, and Gordon J. Curphy, *Leadership: Enhancing the Lessons of Experience* (Homewood, IL: Richard D. Irwin, 1993).

Jamieson, Kathleen Hall, *Civility in the House of Representatives: The 105th Congress* (Philadelphia: Annenberg Public Policy Center, 1999).

Jefferson, Thomas, *Writings,* Library of America, ed. Merrill D. Peterson (New York: Literary Classics of the United States, 1984).

Josipovici, Gabriel, *On Trust: Art and the Temptations of Suspicion* (New Haven, CT: Yale University Press, 1999).

Just, Ward, *Echo House* (New York: Mariner Books, 1997).

Kramer, Roderick M. and Tom R. Tyler, *Trust in Organizations: Frontiers of Theory and Research* (Thousand Oaks, CA: Sage Publications, 1996).

Landy, Marc K., Marc J. Roberts, and Stephen R. Thomas, *The Environmental Protection Agency: Asking the Wrong Questions From Nixon to Clinton* (New York: Oxford University Press, 1994).

Locke, John, *The Second Treatise of Government,* ed. Thomas P. Peardon (Indianapolis, IN: Bobbs-Merrill Company, [1690] 1952).

Lowi, Theodore J., *The End of Liberalism: The Second Republic of the United States,* Second Edition (New York: W.W. Norton and Company, 1979).

Macedo, Stephen, *Liberal Virtues: Citizenship, Virtue, and Community in Liberal Constitutionalism* (Oxford: Clarendon Press, 1990).

Machiavelli, Niccolo, *Discourses on Livy,* trans. Harvey C. Mansfield and Nathan Tarcov (Chicago: University of Chicago Press, [1531] 1996).

Machiavelli, Niccolo, *The Prince,* trans. Harvey C. Mansfield, Jr. (Chicago: University of Chicago Press, [1532] 1985).

Madison, James, *Writings,* Library of America, ed. Jack N. Rakove (New York: Literary Classics of the United States, 1999).

Madison, James, Alexander Hamilton, and John Jay, *The Federalist Papers,* ed. Isaac Kramnick (New York: Penguin Books, [1788] 1987).

March, James G. and Johan P. Olsen, *Rediscovering Institutions: The Organizational Basis of Politics* (New York: Free Press, 1989), 27–28.

Masters, Roger D., *Fortune is a River: Leonardo da Vinci and Niccolo Machiavelli's Magnificent Dream to Change the Course of Florentine History* (New York: Penguin Putnam, 1999).

McLaughlin, Jack, *Jefferson and Monticello: The Biography of a Builder* (New York: Henry Holt and Company, 1988).

Melnick, R. Shep, *Regulation and the Courts: The Case of the Clean Air Act* (Washington, DC: Brookings Institution, 1983).

Miller, William Lee, *Lincoln's Virtue: An Ethical Biography* (New York: Alfred A. Knopf, 2002).

Montesquieu, *The Spirit of the Laws,* eds. Anne Cohler, Basia Miller, and Harold Stone (Cambridge: Cambridge University Press, [1748] 1995).

Morris, Dick, *The New Prince: Machiavelli Updated for the Twenty-First Century* (Los Angeles: Renaissance Books, 1999).

Morris, Edmund, *Theodore Rex* (New York: Random House, 2001).

Muller, Jerry Z., *Adam Smith in His Time and Ours: Designing the Decent Society* (Princeton, NJ: Princeton University Press, 1993).

Neustadt, Richard E., *Presidential Power and the Modern Presidents: The Politics of Leadership from Roosevelt to Reagan* (New York: The Free Press, 1991).

Newton, Isaac, trans. I. Bernard Cohen and Anne Whitman, *The Principia: Mathematical Principles of Natural Philosophy* (Berkeley: University of California Press, [1687] 1999).

Nye, Joseph S., Jr., Philip D. Zelikow, and David C. King, eds., *Why People Don't Trust Government* (Cambridge, MA: Harvard University Press, 1997).

Pennock, J. Roland, *Democratic Political Theory* (Princeton, NJ: Princeton University Press, 1979).

Peterson, Merrill D., *The Jefferson Image in the American Mind* (New York: Oxford University Press, 1960).

Putnam, Robert D., *Bowling Alone: The Collapse and Revival of American Community* (New York: Simon & Schuster, 2000).

Rauch, Jonathan, *Demosclerosis: The Silent Killer of American Government* (New York: Times Books, 1994).

Rawls, John, *A Theory of Justice* (Cambridge, MA: Belknap Press, 1971).

Rawls, John, *Political Liberalism* (New York: Columbia University Press, 1996).

Reich, Robert B., ed., *The Power of Public Ideas* (Cambridge, MA: Harvard University Press, 1990).

Rosenbach, William E. and Robert L. Taylor, eds., *Contemporary Issues in Leadership*, second edition (Boulder, CO: Westview Press, 1989).

Ross, Andrew, *The Celebration Chronicles: Life, Liberty, and the Pursuit of Property Value in Disney's New Town* (New York: Ballantine Books, 1999).

Rothschild, Emma, *Adam Smith, Condorcet, and the Enlightenment* (Cambridge, MA: Harvard University Press, 2001).

Russo, Richard, *Nobody's Fool*, (New York: Random House, 1993).

Sandel, Michael J., *Democracy's Discontent: America in Search of a Public Philosophy* (Cambridge, MA: Belknap Press, 1996).

Sandel, Michael J., *Liberalism and the Limits of Justice*, second edition (New York: Cambridge University Press, 1998).

Schlesinger, Arthur M., Jr., *The Cycles of American History* (Boston: Houghton Mifflin, 1986).

Schoenbrod, David, *Power Without Responsibility: How Congress Abuses the People Through Delegation* (New Haven, CT: Yale University Press, 1993).

Schwartz, Bernard, *Administrative Law* (Boston, MA: Little, Brown and Company, 1976).

Seligman, Adam B., *The Problem of Trust* (Princeton, NJ: Princeton University Press, 1997).

Selznick, Philip, *The Moral Commonwealth: Social Theory and the Promise of Community* (Berkeley: University of California Press, 1994).

Shakespeare, William, *Julius Caesar*, ed. David Daniell (Walton-on-Thames, Surrey: Thomas Nelson and Sons, [1623] 1998).

Smith, Adam, *The Wealth of Nations*, ed. Andrew Skinner (Baltimore, Maryland: Penguin Books, [1776] 1970).

Smith, Adam, *An Inquiry into the Nature and Cause of the Wealth of Nations*, eds. R.H. Campbell, A.S. Skinner and W.B. Todd (Oxford: Clarendon Press, [1776] 1976).

Smith, Adam, *The Theory of Moral Sentiments*, eds. D.D. Raphael and A.L. Macfie (Indianapolis, IN: Liberty Fund, Inc., [1759] 1984).

Storing, Herbert J., *What the Anti-Federalists Were For: The Political Thought of the Opponents of the Constitution* (Chicago: University of Chicago Press, 1981).

Strauss, Leo, *What Is Political Philosophy? And Other Studies* (Westport, CT: Greenwood Press, [1959] 1973).

Sunstein, Cass R., *One Case at a Time: Judicial Minimalism on the Supreme Court* (Cambridge, MA: Harvard University Press, 1999).

Uslaner, Eric M., *The Decline of Comity in Congress* (Ann Arbor: University of Michigan Press, 1993).

Walzer, Michael, *Spheres of Justice: A Defense of Pluralism and Equality* (New York: Basic Books, 1983).

Warren, Mark E., ed., *Democracy and Trust* (Cambridge: Cambridge University Press, 1999).

Washington, George, *Writings,* Library of America, ed. John Rhodehamel (New York: Literary Classics of the United States, 1997).

Willner, Ann Ruth, *The Spellbinders: Charismatic Political Leadership* (New Haven, CT: Yale University Press, 1984).

Wills, Garry, *A Necessary Evil: A History of American Distrust of Government* (New York: Simon & Schuster, 1999).

Wills, Garry, *Explaining America: The Federalist* (Garden City, NY: Doubleday, 1981).

Wills, Garry, *Inventing America: Jefferson's Declaration of Independence* (Garden City, NY: Doubleday, 1978).

Wolfe, Alan, *Whose Keeper? Social Science and Moral Obligation* (Berkeley: University of California Press, 1989).

Wood, Gordon S., *The Radicalism of the American Revolution* (New York: Alfred A. Knopf, 1992).

Wright, Robert, *The Moral Animal: Why We Are the Way We Are: The New Science of Evolutionary Psychology* (New York: Vintage Books, 1994).

Wright, Robert, *Nonzero The Logic of Human Destiny* (New York: Vintage Books, 2000).

B. ARTICLES

Anderson, Elizabeth, 'Beyond Homo Economicus: New Developments in Theories of Social Norms,' *Philosophy & Public Affairs*, 29, 2 (Spring 2000), 170–200.

Aranson, Peter H., Ernest Gelhorn and Glen O. Robinson, 'A Theory of Legislative Delegation,' *Cornell Law Review*, 68 (1982), 1–67.

Berlin, Isaiah, 'The Pursuit of the Ideal,' in I. Berlin, *The Proper Study of Mankind: An Anthology of Essays* (New York: Farrar, Straus and Giroux, 1998), 1–16.

Berlin, Isaiah, 'Two Concepts of Liberty,' in I. Berlin, *The Proper Study of Mankind: An Anthology of Essays* (New York: Farrar, Straus and Giroux, 1998), 191–242.

Berlin, Isaiah, 'The Originality of Machiavelli,' in I. Berlin, *The Proper Study of Mankind: An Anthology of Essays* (New York: Farrar, Straus and Giroux, 1998), 269–325.

Berkowitz, Peter, 'The Futility of Utility,' *The New Republic* (June 5, 2000), 38.

Ciulla, Joanne B., 'Leadership Ethics: Mapping the Territory,' *Business Ethics Quarterly*, 5, 1 (January 1995), 5–28.

Cranston, Maurice, 'Montesquieu,' in Paul Edwards, ed., *The Encyclopedia of Philosophy,* Vol. 5, (New York: Macmillan, 1972), 368–371.

Davis, Kenneth Culp, 'A New Approach to Delegation,' *University of Chicago Law Review*, 36 (1969), 713–733.

Diggs, B.J., 'The Common Good as Reason for Political Action,' *Ethics*, 83, 4 (July 1973), 283–293.

Dowd, Maureen, 'The $7 Million Man,' *New York Times* (July 16, 2000), 15 (wk.).

Dunn, John, 'The Concept of "Trust" in the Politics of John Locke,' in Richard Rorty, J.B. Schneewind, and Quentin Skinner, eds., *Philosophy in History: Essays on the Historiography of Philosophy* (Cambridge: Cambridge University Press, 1984), 279–301.

Dworkin, Ronald, 'Liberal Community,' *California Law Review,* 77 (May 1989), 479–504.

Epstein, Richard, 'Through the Smog: What the Court Actually Ruled,' *Wall Street Journal*, 237 (March 1, 2001) A22.

Farrell, Alex and Maureen Hart, 'What Does Sustainability Really Mean? The Search for Useful Indicators,' *Environment*, 40, 9 (November 1998), 4–9, 26–31.

Galston, William A., 'Political Knowledge, Political Engagement, and Civic Education,' *Annual Review of Political Science,* 4 (2001), 217–234.

Hulliung, Mark, 'Montesquieu, Charles Louis De Secondat,' in Edward Craig, ed., *Routledge Encyclopedia of Philosophy*, Vol. 6 (London: Routledge, 1998), 489–494.

Jackman, Robert W. and Ross A. Miller, 'Social Capital and Politics,' *Annual Review of Political Science* 1 (1998), 47–73.

Kant, Immanuel, 'Idea for a Universal History from a Cosmopolitan Point of view,' in Ernst Behler, ed., *Philosophical Writings* (New York: Continuum, 1986) 249–262.

Kellog, Alex P., 'Looking Inward, Freshmen Care Less About Politics and More About Money,' *Chronicle of Higher Education* (January 26, 2001), A47.

Kramnick, Isaac, 'Introduction,' in Isaac Kramnick, ed., *The Federalist Papers* (New York: Penguin Books, 1987) 16–28.

Lawson, Gary, 'The Rise and Fall of the Administrative State,' *Harvard Law Review*, 107 (1994), 1231–1254.

Lutz, Donald S., 'The Relative Influence of European Writers on Late Eighteenth Century American Political Thought,' *American Political Science Review*, 78 (1984), 189–198.

Mandeville, Bernard, 'Grumbling Hive: or, Knaves, Turn'd Honest,' in Frederick Benjamin Kaye, ed., *The Fable of the Bees: or, Private Vices, Publick Benefits* (Oxford: The Clarendon Press, [1705] 1924), 24–25.

Mills, Claudia, '"Not a Mere Modus Vivendi:" The Bases for Allegiance to the Just State,' in Victoria Davion and Clark Wolf, eds., *The Idea of a Political Liberalism: Essays on Rawls* (Lanham, MD: Rowman & Littlefield Publishers, 2000), 190–203.

Morin, Richard and Don Balz, 'Americans Losing Trust in Each Other and Institutions,' *Washington Post* (January 28, 1996) A1, A6.

Nye, Joseph S., Jr., 'Introduction: The Decline of Confidence in Government,' in Joseph Nye, Philip D. Zelihow and David C. King, eds., *Why People Don't Trust Government* (Cambridge, MA: Harvard University Press, 1997) 1–18.

Pollon, Michael, 'Town-Building is No Mickey Mouse Operation,' *New York Times Magazine* (December 14, 1997), 58, 78.

Putnam, Robert D., 'Bowling Alone: America's Declining Social Capital,' *Journal of Democracy,* 6 (January 1995), 65–78.

Putnam, Robert D., '"The Prosperous Community" Social Capital and Public Life,' *American Prospect*, 13 (Spring 1993), 35–42.

Putnam, Robert D., 'The Strange Disappearance of Civic America,' *American Prospect* 24 (Winter 1996), 34–48.

Riley, Jonathan, 'Interpreting Berlin's Liberalism,' *American Political Science Review,* 95, 2 (June 2001), 283–295.

Ruscio, Kenneth P., 'Jay's Pirouette, or Why Political Trust is Not the Same as Personal Trust,' *Administration & Society*, 31, 5 (November 1999), 639–657.

Ruscio, Kenneth P., 'Trust, Democracy, and Public Management: A Theoretical Argument,' *Journal of Public Administration Research and Theory*, 6, 3 (July 1996), 461–477.

Ruscio, Kenneth P., 'Trust in the Administrative State,' *Public Administration Review*, 57, 5 (September/October 1997), 454–458.

Ryan, Alan, 'Isaiah Berlin: Political Theory and Liberal Culture,' *Annual Review of Political Science*, 2 (1999), 345–362.

Saari, Donald G. and Katie K. Sieberg, 'The Sum of the Parts Can Violate the Whole,' *American Political Science Review*, 95, 2 (June 2001), 415–433.

Sandel, Michael J., 'Review of Political Liberalism,' *Harvard Law Review*, 107 (1994), 1765–1794.

Shapiro, Martin, 'Administrative Discretion: The Next Stage,' *Yale Law Journal*, 92 (1983), 1487–1522.

Shklar, Judith N., 'The Liberalism of Fear,' in Stanley Hoffmann, ed., *Political Thought and Political Thinkers* (Chicago: University of Chicago Press, 1998), 3–20.

Shklar, Judith N., 'Montesquieu and the New Republicanism,' in Stanley Hoffmann, ed., *Political Thought and Political Thinkers* (Chicago: University of Chicago Press, 1998), 244–261.

Starobin, Paul, 'The Bradley Question,' *National Journal*, 31 (August 21, 1999).

Summers, Lawrence, 'Let Them Eat Pollution,' *The Economist* (February 8, 1992), 66.

Sundquist, James L., 'The Crisis of Competence in Our National Government,' *Political Science Quarterly*, 95, 2 (Summer 1980), 186.

Sunstein, Cass R., 'Agreement Without Theory,' in Stephen Macedo, ed., *Deliberative Politics: Essays on Democracy and Disagreement* (New York: Oxford University Press, 1999), 123–150.

Sunstein, Cass R., 'Is the Clean Air Act Unconstitutional?,' *Michigan Law Review*, 98 (November 1999), 303–394.

Sunstein, Cass R., 'Non-delegation Canons,' *University of Chicago Law Review*, 67, 2 (Spring 2000), 315–343.

Thompson, Dennis F., 'Bureaucracy and Democracy,' in Graeme Duncan, ed., *Democratic Theory and Practice* (Cambridge: Cambridge University Press, 1983), 235–250.

Thompson, Dennis F., 'Mediated Corruption: The Case of the Keating Five,' *American Political Science Review*, 87, 2 (June 1993), 369–381.

Uslaner, Eric M., 'Producing and Consuming Trust,' *Political Science Quarterly*, 115, 4 (2000–01), 569–590.

Verba, Sidney, 'The 1993 James Madison Award Lecture: The Voice of the People,' *PS: Political Science and Politics*, 26 (December 1993), 677–686.

Warren, Mark E., 'Democratic Theory and Trust,' in Mark E. Warren, ed., *Democracy and Trust* (Cambridge: Cambridge University Press, 1995), 310–345.

Weaver, David R., 'Leadership, Locke, and the Federalist,' *American Journal of Political Science*, 41, 2 (April 1997), 425.

Weaver, David R., 'Liberalism and Leadership: Lockean Roots,' *Leadership Quarterly*, 2, 3 (Fall 1991), 157–174.

Williamson, Oliver E., 'Calculativeness, Trust, and Economic Organization,' *Journal of Law and Economics*, 36 (April 1993), 486.

Wilson, James Q., 'Interests and Deliberation in the American Republic, or, Why James Madison Would Never Have Received the James Madison Award,' *PS: Political Science and Politics*, 23, 4 (December 1990), 558–562.

Wolfe, Alan, 'Make Nice, Not War,' *Wall Street Journal*, 231 (April 28, 1998), A16.

Wood, Gordon S., 'Interests and Disinterestedness in the Making of the Constitution,' in Richard Beeman, Stephen Botein, and Edward C. Carter II, eds., *Beyond Confederation: Origins of the Constitution and American National Identity* (Chapel Hill: University of North Carolina Press, 1987), 69–109.

C.   PUBLIC STATUTES AND CASES

American Trucking Association, Inc. et al., *v.* United States EPA, 175 F. 3d 1027 (1999) (2-1 decision) (Tatel dissenting) and 195 F. 3d 4 (1999).

Chevron *v.* National Resources Defense Council, 467 US 837, 843 (1984).

The Federal Administrative Procedure Act, 60 Stat 237 (1946).

Mistretta *v.* United States, 488 US 372 (1989).

Panama Refining Company *v.* Ryan, 293 US 399 (1935).

Schecter Poultry Corporation *v.* United States, 295 US 495 (1935).

Whitman *v.* American Trucking, 531 US 457 (2001) (Thomas concurring).

Whitman *v.* American Trucking, Transcripts of oral arguments of General Seth P. Waxman, Edward W. Warren, Esq., and Judith L. French, Esq.

D. OTHER WORKS

'A Nation of Spectators: How Civic Disengagement Weakens America and What We Can Do About It,' *Final Report of the National Commission on Civic Renewal*, University of Maryland, 1999.

Bush, George, Jr., 'Inaugural Address,' *Weekly Compilation of Presidential Documents*, Vol. 37, No. 4 (Online: January 29, 2001), Available: http://www.access.gpo.gov/nara/v37no4.html, [July 27, 2001].

Carter, Jimmy, 'Administration of Jimmy Carter: Farewell Address to the Nation,' *Public Papers of the Presidents, 1980–81*, Vol. III, (GPO, 1982), 2889–2893.

Cranston, Sen., (CA), 'Cranston Response to Rudman Statement,' *Congressional Record* (Online: December 18, 1991), Available: http://thomas.loc.gov, [October 15, 2000].

Danforth, John, 'What is the Point of Serving?,' excerpt from remarks on the Senate Floor, *Washington Post* (March 28, 1992), A20.

Sashkin, Marshall and W.E. Rosenbach, 'Visionary Leadership Theory: A Current Overview Model, Measures, and Research,' working paper 9–114, George Washington University, Graduate School of Education and Human Development (1998), 5–20.

U.S. Constitution, Preamble.

Index